Praise for *UX for Beginners*

"There are many books about UX but few dare to take on the entire spectrum of UX work. UX for Beginners does that and does it well. With digestible chunks of insight into the many facets of UX and design, it gives the beginner a broad view into the field, encouraging them to dig deeper into the areas where they are most passionate."

-Jeff Gothelf
Author of *Lean UX*

"The UX field is a vast field with so much to learn. If you're just getting started, the learning curve seems daunting.

In this practical book, Joel Marsh bends the UX learning curve back to earth providing practical lessons that will give you a solid start in the UX field."

-Aarron Walter
VP of R&D at MailChimp, author of *Designing for Emotion*

"There are a lot of methods, materials and myths about the field of User Experience. UX for Beginners offers an approachable format and plenty of pointers to start making sense of it all."

-Jeff Sauro
Principal UX Researcher & Statistical Analyst, MeasuringU

"The UX Crash Course is the most amazing thing in the history of amazing things. No hyperbole. Thanks, Joel."

-Silvestre Tanenbaum
Aspiring UX designer

UX for Beginners

Joel Marsh

Illustrations by Jose Marzan, Jr.

Beijing · Boston · Farnham · Sebastopol · Tokyo

UX for Beginners

by Joel Marsh

Copyright © 2016 Joel Marsh. All rights reserved.

Printed in the United States of America.

Published by O'Reilly Media, Inc., 1005 Gravenstein Highway North, Sebastopol, CA 95472.

O'Reilly books may be purchased for educational, business, or sales promotional use. Online editions are also available for most titles (*oreilly.com*). For more information, contact our corporate/institutional sales department: (800) 998-9938 or *corporate@oreilly.com*.

Acquisitions Editor: Nick Lombardi
Developmental Editor: Angela Rufino
Production Editor: Melanie Yarbrough
Copyeditor: Octal Publishing
Proofreader: Amanda Kersey

Indexer: Bob Pfahler
Cover Designer: Ellie Volckhausen
Interior Designers: Ron Bilodeau and Monica Kamsvaag
Illustrator: Jose Marzan Jr.
Compositor: Melanie Yarbrough

Revision History for the First Edition:

2017-11-17	Third release
2018-11-16	Fourth release
2019-04-05	Fifth release
2019-09-20	Sixth release

See *http://oreilly.com/catalog/errata.csp?isbn=0636920035084* for release details.

978-1-491-91268-3

[CD]

Contents

13. Data for Designers

14. Get a Job, You Dirty Hippy

Preface

This Book Truly Practices What It Preaches

It started as an email newsletter, grew into a blog, became viral, and now you have it. The format of the book is based on science and research with real readers. It was then reviewed by some of the industry's leading UXers—all to make it as engaging and useful as possible. We even gathered feedback from the Internet while we were writing it!

This Book Exists Because It Is Needed

(i.e., My "user research" uncovered a problem.)

Originally, these lessons were an email newsletter. Throughout my time working with startups, famous global brands, and in-house product teams, I was asked the same basic UX questions over and over, everywhere I worked. So, I decided to start a newsletter of *UX ProTips*, for my coworkers.

Once a week, I would write a short, funny lesson about one simple UX thing and email it to the company. These people were busy, and not experts, and they needed to be entertained if I expected them to learn about *someone else's job (mine)*.

In other words, they were beginners.

At first, I was worried about seeming arrogant or annoying, but everybody loved it! They even started sending me questions to answer. It didn't take long before I started hearing my answers being repeated to clients in meetings, and people outside of our company would reply, asking how they could subscribe!

Soon after that, I noticed that the most popular question in UX forums was "What should I read to get started in UX?" And thus, my ProTips became a blog: *www.TheHipperElement.com*. My first big project for the blog was the *UX Crash Course*. Thirty-one daily lessons about the most fundamental things in UX, which I posted every day in January, 2014. It was a huge success. Much bigger than expected. That Crash Course has now been read over a million times without paying a cent for promotion.

That blog is the motivation for this book. And if you want even more proof that there was a need, consider this: we were able to use the title *UX for Beginners* because it had never been used! And we're talking about a job that was ranked fourteenth on a list of the most in-demand jobs in America in 2015!

Who Is This Book For?

(i.e., My "user profiles")

Even if you still don't understand what I mean by "UX"— it's short for User eXperience, by the way—you're in the right place. This book is written for *three types of people*: non-designers who want to become designers, managers of UX designers, and experienced people from other jobs who want to learn more about UX.

If you're a non-designer, this book is specifically for you. My mission is to create more designers by teaching the fundamentals in a simple way—something that is surprisingly hard to find. This isn't just a book about "thinking like a designer" or "the UX mentality," it is a practical set of lessons that teach what to *do; how to be a UX designer* on the first day of your first job. If you're a student, or an intern, or a recent graduate that feels intimidated by doing UX "for real," welcome. We need you.

If you manage UX designers, you're either a designer yourself or you have the authority to enable or disable the designers on your team. Either way, the more time you spend *managing* design, the less time you spend *doing* design, so a refresher is always useful, especially an easy, funny one like this. But, more important, being a manager also means that you are in a position to *teach UX*, and this book has been created for that reason, too. Use it as a reference or as a way to kick-start conversations with your team. Sometimes the most valuable thing is a good book that backs you up.

And finally, you might have experience in something relevant, like programming, or project management, or sales, but now you need to know more about UX design. Thanks for realizing that UX is a core element in all digital products and services! This book is a great place for you to initiate yourself and learn to "talk the talk" while building a solid understanding of the people who "walk the walk." And if you aspire to go *sideways* into a design position in the future, fantastic!

How the Book Is Structured

(i.e., The "Information Architecture" of this book)

There are 100 lessons, grouped into sections, and they roughly follow the real process of doing UX on a real project. So if you are sitting at your first UX job right now, just start reading and it will feel like we're working on it together. Also, try not to laugh too loud at my jokes, people will think you're a weirdo.

You won't find any long case studies, or complex diagrams, or chapters that do a "deep dive" on a specific topic. This book is designed to be a quick-and-dirty introduction to User Experience design. The lessons are short, and did I mention how funny and modest I am?

Although it's quick, this book covers *a lot*. It may not be *every* UX-related topic in the world, but it introduces plenty. I have specifically focused on things that a *beginner* needs, so more advanced ideas like *iteration* or "lean" and "agile" processes, or *contextual* design, or *design critiques*, or *accessibility* and stuff like that are not covered in detail. That's for designers with more experience. You can Google those things or read one of the other fine books that O'Reilly offers on those subjects.

All of the 100 lessons are self-contained: you don't have to read them in order if you don't want to. If there is something special you want to learn or if you want to keep it on your desk as a reference, do it! It's also great to just have "around" for people to read on a coffee break.

The lessons are grouped into 14 sections:

- First, in the section called *Key Ideas*, you will learn some basic concepts. UX design can be counterintuitive some-times, and a lot of your "common sense" will lead you in the wrong direction. If you have never designed anything before, take the time to read each of those lessons and think about them before continuing.

- In the section called *Before You Start*, you'll learn some practical stuff that will prepare you for conversations later in the process. If you work in a big company, those parts will bite you in the ass if you skip them.

- In *Behavior Basics, User Research*, and *The Limits of Our Minds*, you will learn the fundamentals of understanding how and why humans do what they do, and how to investigate when your users do something you don't expect.

- The sections *Information Architecture* and *Designing Behavior* start to combine the basic ideas from the previous sections into your *craft*. The process and science of User Experience design. For a lot of people that might be a whole new way of thinking about design in general.

Then you start to actually design things:

- *Visual Design Principles* come *before* the *Wireframing & Prototypes* in this book, because *making good wire-frames*—your main document as a UX designer—requires an understanding of how design *works*, not just what it looks like. After you understand how the size, color, and layout of your design can influence the user, you will learn how to make wireframes, and how *not* to make wireframes.

- In *Psychology of Usability* and *Content*, you will learn how to make your designs *feel* easier and more persuasive, so more people will use them.

- *The Moment of Truth* is critical: the launch.

- After the launch, any good UX designer will *measure* how their design works in the real world, with real users. You'll learn about that in the section called *Data for Designers*. Don't worry, there are no equations or anything… it's mostly pictures. ;)

- And finally, in *Get A Job You Dirty Hippy*, you'll learn a few things about what UX role is right for you, what should be in your portfolio, and what you might actually *do* all day at your first design job.

We even threw in some amazing illustrations to make it more visual, easier to understand, more fun, and because every great author needs a few rubber ducks to get their point across. Obviously.

"*I always include rubber ducks. Always.*"—Ernest Hemingway

The Main Goals of this Book

Like any good UX project, this book has two goals:

- To make more UX designers
- To make me a millionaire

In other words, a *user* goal and a *business* goal.

BUT:

I only achieve goal #2 if I achieve goal #1 in a spectacular way. The better I am at turning you into a great UX designer, the more you will share and discuss this book with others, making even more UX designers, and giving me the funds I need to finally have a llama farm in my backyard.

Every designer's dream, am I right?

So I needed to make this book a great experience for *you* if I really want to start my million-dollar llama empire. If I succeed, we both win. If I fail, we both lose. That's the way

UX should be. Some people call that "empathy." I just think it's how good product design works.

If you think the book could be better in any way, or if you have a story about how it helped you be a better designer, please tell me on Twitter: *@JoelMarsh*

And seriously, share this book with someone if you like it. Those llamas aren't going to feed themselves.

Enjoy!

Acknowledgements

This book could not have been made without the UX community itself, my most curious students, my most talented interns, and every colleague I have had over the past decade or so. Their questions, feedback, interest, and general lack of attention span (haha) have all come together in this book and the work related to it.

Thanks to my girlfriend, Camilla, for dealing with all the mornings when I got up to write a daily UX Crash Course lesson (and therefore barely spoke to her), and to my friends for not rolling their eyes when I begin a sentence with "On my blog…" or "In my book…"

I would also like to acknowledge anyone and everyone who actually takes the time to be a really good UX designer, whether you start here or not.

We, my friends, are defining the future in real time.

Key Ideas

What Is UX?

The best place to start any education is at the beginning.

Everything has a user experience. Your job is not to create the user experience. Your job is to make it good.

And what do I mean by "good" user experience? It is common to think that a good user experience is one that makes users happy.

Not true!

If happiness was your only goal, you could just throw in some *Lolcats* and random *compliments* and go home. But—although that's not the worst universe I can imagine—your boss may not be satisfied with the results. The goal of a UX designer is to make users effective.

A user's experience is just the tip of the iceberg:

Many people mistakenly think that "UX" means a *user's experience*, but it is actually about "doing" the process of User Experience Design. A user's individual experience is their conscious, subjective opinion of your app or site. User feedback is important—sometimes—but UX designers need to do a lot more than that.

"Doing" UX

UX Design (also sometimes called UXD) involves a process very *similar to doing science*: you do research to understand the users, you develop ideas to solve the users' needs—and the needs of the business—and you build and measure those solutions in the real world to see if they work.

You will learn about all of that in this book. Or if that's not your deal, Lolcats are still an option.

The Five Main Ingredients of UX

User Experience design is a process, and these lessons roughly follow that process, but you should always keep these five things in mind: *Psychology, Usability, Design, Copywriting,* and *Analysis*.

Any one of these five ingredients could be a book of its own, so I will be oversimplifying a bit. This is supposed to be a crash course, not Wikipedia.

Although, to be fair, I'm pretty sure *Wikipedia's UX page* was written by a guy who heard about UX once… at that thing… that time…

1. Psychology

    A user's mind is complex. You should know; you have one, (I assume). UXers work with subjective thoughts and feelings a lot; they can make or break your results. And the designer must ignore their own psychology sometimes, too, and that's hard!

Ask yourself:

   – What is the user's motivation to be here in the first place?

   – How does this make them feel?

   – How much work does the user have to do to get what they want?

   – What habits are created if they do this over and over?

   – What do they expect when they click this?

   – Are you assuming they know something that they haven't learned yet?

   – Is this something they want to do again? Why? How often?

   – Are you thinking of the user's wants and needs, or your own?

   – How are you rewarding good behavior?

2. Usability

If user psychology is mostly subconscious, usability is mostly conscious. You know when something is confusing. There are cases where it is more fun if something is hard—like a game—but for everything else, we want it to be so easy that even a (moron) could use it.

Ask yourself:

- Could you get the job done with less input from the user?

- Are there any user mistakes you could prevent? (Hint: Yes, there are.)

- Are you being clear and direct, or is this a little too clever?

- Is it easy to find (good), hard to miss (better), or subconsciously expected (best)?

- Are you working with the user's assumptions or against them?

- Have you provided everything the user needs to know?

- Could you solve this just as well by doing something more common?

- Are you basing your decisions on your own logic or categories, or the user's intuition? How do you know?

- If the user doesn't read the fine print, does it still work/make sense?

3. Design

As the UX designer, your definition of "design" will be much less artistic than a lot of designers. Whether you "like it" is irrelevant. In UX, design is how it works, and it's something you can prove; it's not a matter of style.

Ask yourself:

- Do users think it looks good? Do they trust it immediately?

- Does it communicate the purpose and function without words?

- Does it represent the brand? Does it all feel like the same site?

- Does the design lead the user's eyes to the right places? How do you know?

- Do the colors, shapes, and typography help people find what they want and improve usability of the details?

- Do clickable things look different than nonclickable things?

4. Copywriting

There is a huge difference between writing brand copy (text) and writing UX copy. Brand copy supports the image and values of the company. UX copy gets shit done as directly and simply as possible.

Ask yourself:

- Does it sound confident and tell the user what to do?

- Does it motivate the user to complete their goal? Is that what we want?

- Is the biggest text the most important text? Why not?

- Does it inform the user or does it assume that they already understand?

- Does it reduce anxiety?

- Is it clear, direct, simple, and functional?

5. Analysis

In my opinion, most designers' weak spot is analysis. But we can fix that! Analysis is the main thing that separates UX from other types of design, and it makes you extremely valuable. It literally pays to be good at it.

So, ask yourself:

- Are you using data to prove that you are right, or to learn the truth?

- Are you looking for subjective opinions or objective facts?

- Have you collected information that can give you those types of answers?

- Do you know why users do that, or are you interpreting their behavior?

- Are you looking at absolute numbers, or relative improvements?

- How will you measure this? Are you measuring the right things?

- Are you looking for bad results, too? Why not?

- How can you use this analysis to make improvements?

Your Perspective

In User Experience design, the way you look at a problem can make or break your work. Your own desires and experience can even work against the users.

Know Thyself

There are two things you need to be aware of, about yourself, before you can start understanding users well:

- You want things that don't matter to users.
- You know things that don't matter to users.

Meditate on that for a minute.

Namasté.

Empathy: Want What They Want

If there is one word that is over-sold in UX, it's "*empathy*". It *is* important though. It is. In general, and in UX.

But here's a secret: unless you are a serial killer, you have empathy. If you are a serial killer, UX design might not be for you. What we want by nature might not be what the users want. And that's a big deal. It means your intuition about the users might be wrong!

Do research. Talk to users. Study the data. Cuddle some puppies. When you truly understand a problem, it becomes your problem, emotionally. That's empathy. You will feel it. A good solution will excite you. Not because you're an emotional superhero, but because you relate to the users.

You're one of them now.

single tear

Ask yourself:

- If you have to choose between a feature for your users or having this design in your portfolio, what will you choose?
- If users don't like your design, what would probably be the reason?
- Have you actually tried the software, or are you just clicking "next" to get through it?

You Know Too Much

Designing for people who know less than you is a core part of UX.

Not people who are dumber than you. People who *know less*.

You know that your site gets more powerful if you customize it, but users don't. You know that your menu categories match the teams in your company, but users don't. And you know your prices are high because licensing fees make your content expensive to make, but users don't.

If users don't know, users don't care. And sometimes even when they *do* know, they don't care! Licensing fees? That's your problem. They can get a pirated copy for free.

Ask yourself:

- If you didn't read the text, would you understand?
- If a user only had a few clicks to find what they want, would this design be *your* best bet?

- Are you judging a feature based on the time it will take to build it or the value to the user?
- Are you assuming users will click it just because it exists? (They won't.)

The Three "Whats" of User Perspective

Ah, finally! It's time to discuss the user's mind, and it's always good to start with the basics and build from there.

A good design communicates three things:

1. What is this?
2. What is the benefit for the user?
3. What should they do next?

"What Is This?"

It is always a good idea to have a title or an image (or both) that answers the question: "what is this?" Seems pretty basic, right? But it's amazing how many websites forget to do it. Why? Because *we* already know. But the user doesn't. Is it an article? A registration form? A party for people who love lemons? A place to see goats? Your gerbil's secret YouTube channel?

Just tell them. Directly. And use simple words. Nobody is excited when you pull out the dictionary at a party. Especially not a lemon party.

"What's in It for Me?"

This is the "why" of user experience. What can the user gain?

It is better to show users what they will get, rather than tell them. You can use a video, demo, example images, free trial, sample content, testimonials, or several of those things!

The best answers to "what is it?" also tell you a little about what you get. For example, "A global network of megalomaniacs cooperating to conquer the world and share funny cat pics." That tells you what it is, and what you get (assuming you're a megalomaniac who loves cats).

REMEMBER

You're saying what's in it for them. Not why you want them to register/buy/click.

User motivation is a thousand times more valuable than beauty or usability—for the company—but how much time do you spend talking about it at work?

"What Do I Do?"

If the user understands what it is and they are motivated to know or see more, their next action should be obvious in your design.

It could be something small, like "What do I click now?" or "How do I register?"

It could be something bigger, like "How do I get started?" or "How do I buy?" or "Where do I get more training?"

There is always a "next" step. Sometimes there are a few possibilities. It's up to you to figure out what the users might need, and tell them how to get it.

Solutions versus Ideas

UX designers must be creative every day. But our definition of creativity is less artistic and more analytical than some other designers. If you're not solving problems, you're not doing UX.

All types of designers work with ideas. And great ideas are great!

Ideas come in different flavors. Some ideas are things we would like to make, like, perhaps, a fish-and-chocolate soufflé. ("I love both of those things! They must be great together!"). Some ideas are meaningful to us in a personal way, like that tattoo that reminds you of your pet hamster, Chewy. God rest his soul. And some ideas are solutions to problems. That's what UX is all about.

Solutions are ideas with meaning for other people.

Unlike most artists and designers, UX designers do not focus on the ideas that have meaning for themselves. You should care a lot about creativity, but if your ideas are not meaningful for other people—the users—then they are not meaningful for you.

That means you have to spend a lot of time trying to understand problems that mean nothing to you. And that might feel unnatural at first. That's why UX is a unique, valuable job: it's tricky.

Solutions are ideas that can be wrong.

In UX, we can test things. We can design more than one solution to the same problem and see which one is better. And we can ask users which solution they prefer.

This means that UX is a special kind of design: it can be *wrong*. And we can *prove* that it is wrong.

And the same solution can be right for one site, and wrong for another! Just because Twitter does it, doesn't mean it's right for you.

The Pyramid of UX Impact

UX is a lot more than buttons and wireframes. The stuff that seems obvious is only the tip of the iceberg, and the stuff that matters most is completely invisible.

As a UX designer, your job is to *create value*—from the user's perspective. Some parts of the UX process create more value than others. Spend your time wisely. You will learn about every part of the Pyramid throughout the rest of this book. For now, just understand that the bottom of the pyramid—the big layers—are the parts that can destroy a product if you ignore them. And they are often invisible. The top of the pyramid—the small layers—are the parts that might not add value to your product, no matter how much time you spend on them. And they are usually visible.

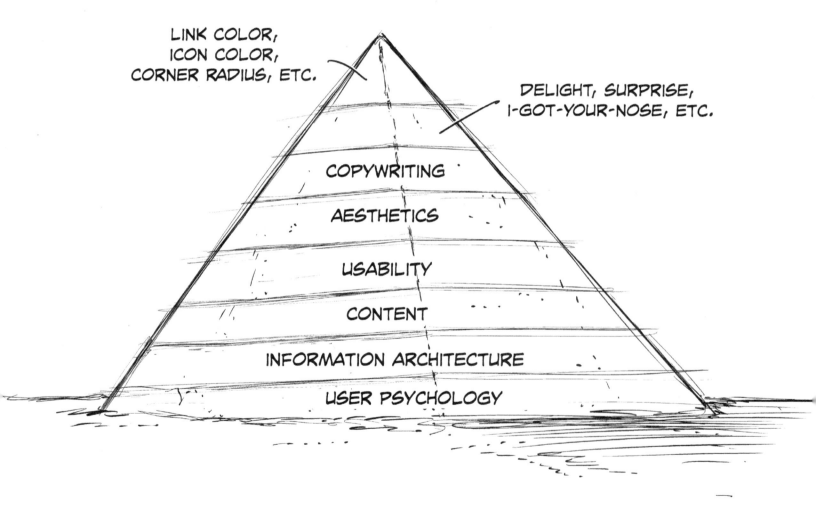

LINK COLOR,
ICON COLOR,
CORNER RADIUS, ETC.

DELIGHT, SURPRISE,
I-GOT-YOUR-NOSE, ETC.

COPYWRITING

AESTHETICS

USABILITY

CONTENT

INFORMATION ARCHITECTURE

USER PSYCHOLOGY

Before You Start

User Goals and Business Goals

When you start a new UX project—before you design anything—
you need to understand your goals. Two of them. And nothing
is more important to your success as a UX designer.

User Goals

Users always want something because they are people, and
people always want something. Whether they are peeking
at an ex on Facebook, trying to find their next ex on a dating
site, or looking for sneezing pandas on YouTube, they want
something.

They might also want to do something productive (or so I am
told). There is a whole section about user research starting on
page 61. For now, just assume you know stuff.

Business Goals

Every organization has a reason for creating a site or app
in the first place. Typically it's money, but it might be brand
awareness, or getting new members for a community, etc.

The specific type of business goal is important. If you want to
show more ads, your UX strategy will be a lot different than if
you want to sell products or promote via social media.

These things are often called "metrics" or "Key Performance
Indicators" (KPIs) by the business-y folks.

Align the goals

The real test of a UX designer is how well you can align those
goals so the business benefits when the user reaches their
goal. (*Not the other way around!*)

YouTube makes money via ads, and users want to find good
videos. Therefore, putting ads in the videos, or on the same
page, makes sense. But, more than that, making it easy to
search for videos and find similar videos will get users to
watch more, which makes YouTube more money.

If the goals are *not* aligned, you will have one of two problems: either users can get what they want *without* helping
the business (lots of users, no success), or the users don't get
what they want (no users, no success).

If YouTube made you watch 20 minutes of ads for every 30 seconds of videos, it would die a quick, painful death. Ain't nobody got time fo' dat. But a few seconds of ads is a small price to pay for those sweet, sweet sneezing pandas.

UX Is a Process

Every company is different. Every team is different. And every designer is different. So it's worth asking some questions about how you work.

You will hear the word "process" a lot when people talk about design. It even comes up a few times in this book.

I often say things like, "UX needs to start early in the process," or "A scientific process doesn't allow bad ideas to survive," or "I am in the process of photoshopping my boss' head onto Arnold Schwarzenegger's body right now."

So, you need to understand UX as a *process*.

UX Is Not an Event or a Task

If you ever hear someone talk about UX like it is a one-time thing, or a moment in time, or a task that *someone* needs to do, feel free to interrupt. That's wrong.

A UX designer is not "the person who does the UX part". That's like saying that the water is just the wet part of your drink.

Without the *process* of doing UX, you will have *bad* UX by default. There is no such thing as "no UX." Even shitty products give the user an experience.

The experience of homicidal rage.

You need to get involved in several places, at many times, to design and protect a good user experience.

A Company Has a Process, Too

Your process as a UX designer is for you to gather the information you need, research the users, design the solution, make sure it is implemented properly, and measure the results.

But, the company you work with also has a process to get the whole project done.

UX designers are included in that process, along with the coders, the project managers, the other designers, the strategists, the business people, the assistant managers, the middle managers, the executive managers, the manager's managers, and so on.

At the beginning of a new project or when you get a new job, always learn how the company expects you to fit into the "machine" of production, and try to respect that overall way of working.

Always Question the Process

Your process and *your company's* process have something in common: they can always improve.

Some improvements are easier said than done, but UX is a new part of business in general, so there is a good chance you will need to figure out where UX *should* fit, not just where your company *expects it to fit*.

If you are the first UX person to ever work at a company, you need to have this discussion with your colleagues and managers. The earlier UX can be part of the product process, the better.

If you're just one in a long line of fine UX designers, talk to them and find out how they think the process could be improved and where you would be most valuable.

And if the process just makes your life a living hell—like if they want you to work with something evil called "sprints"—then tell somebody that you're having difficulty! There might be a better way.

If a company's process forces you to do bad work, the process might be wrong for UX.

So speak up!

(Remember: if you fix the process and still do bad work, the problem is not the process.)

Gathering Requirements

In UX, the more you understand what you can't do and what you must do, the better your final designs will be.

In many types of design, part of the process is to find inspiration and generate lots of ideas. Mood boards. Photography. Hallucinogens. Part of *artistic* creativity is to feed your mind with freedom and possibilities.

But that's not how problem-solving works.

As a UX designer, your most ingenious creative ideas will come from the limitations and restrictions you define by studying the problem.

When those limitations come from your own colleagues and previous work, we call them "requirements."

Requirements Protect You from Mistakes

In a real UX job, your design will affect other parts of the company: the sales team, the programmers, the executives.

Always have a discussion with each of the "stakeholders" (important people), from each department that is affected by the design.

Collect problems that could be solved, things that can't be changed, or technical things that *must* be included.

The sales team has products that it needs to sell. The programmers might have code that is hard to change. Executives have long-term goals that must be respected. The janitors… well, they probably won't be affected by your designs, but you could help them out by not leaving your Red Bull cans all over the place. Geez.

By talking with stakeholders, you will avoid making mistakes that could cost time and money. Plus, your desk won't attract so many flies in the summer.

You're a UX designer now; other people's needs are your needs.

Don't Ask Stakeholders for Solutions or Wishes

Be careful not to confuse "requirements" and "expectations."

When someone says they *need* something, ask why. If the answer is something about the opinions or expectations of other people, ask more questions.

Sometimes companies keep working on bad ideas because everyone assumes it can't be better, and that might not be true. Sometimes they add a lot of unnecessary features because nobody said no.

Building Consensus

UX designers often find themselves in the middle of everything and everyone. Therefore, you should prepare yourself to convince a room full of people that your design is right. And have reasons to back it up.

In the previous lesson, we learned about gathering requirements from important people in your company.

But you also have to bring your own information to the discussion. Other people might disagree with your design, and if you can't back it up, why should they believe you?

As a UX designer, you need to have reasons to support your design *before* you design it, and you have to be able to defend your choices.

You might have to *prove* that you are right!

Know Your Craft

Good research, good theory, and good data are persuasive. Build agreement among stakeholders by doing good research, having a solid understanding of the users, their problems, and the goals, and by taking the time to explain important ideas to stakeholders when they don't understand.

And always be the first to suggest an experiment when something is truly subjective. You'll learn more about that in the next lesson, Psychology vs Culture.

If you don't know, you don't know.

DO NOT LIE ABOUT UX. EVER.

If you don't know the answer to a question, admit it, and say you will find out.

There is no room for bullshit in UX.

UX is widely misunderstood, and if your bullshit turns out to be false, the rest of us will want to leave a horse head in your bed. (Not good.)

Lying in UX makes us all look bad. Your opinion isn't better than anyone else's. Make sure your information is.

Behavior Basics

Psychology versus Culture

Some parts of human behavior are predictable. Some aren't. In this lesson, I want to introduce a two-part model that will help you know what you can control and what you can't.

Psychology

We are all born with the same brain (more or less). The details might vary a bit, but overall, it's the same machine.

We can all feel happy and sad. We all want to be respected. We can all learn to ride a bicycle, and we all regret tequila the next day. Pinterest.com, for example, is built on the psychological principle of collecting things we like. That is common to all people.

Psychology, in this sense, is the same for all of us. Most of what we will learn in this book is about psychology. The stuff we all share. Behavior you can predict and use in your designs.

But differences are useful, too.

Culture

After we're born, we take those brains on very different journeys. You might be an Eastern, Christian scientist who climbed Everest, or a Western, atheist artist who watches monster truck videos 24/7.

For example: all people feel the need for justice, but one person might think death row is appropriate and another person might not. Or, to continue our Pinterest example: "collecting" might be universal, but what we collect is highly personal. Pinterest does a lot of work to find topics of interest for each user, whether that is _interfaces_, _architecture_, or _fluffy chickens_.

Culture, in this sense, is different for each of us. People with similar experiences and personalities will have similar cultures, but on an individual level, culture can be almost anything.

The Practical Difference

Psychological elements—such as collecting things you like—can become focused over time as you move toward "optimal" functionality. The "perfect" feature. Their purpose is usually more general, but they have the most impact overall.

Cultural elements—like your topics of interest—will expand over time as users want to personalize or categorize things more and more. They cannot be optimized, only customized. Their purpose is more detailed, but there are more of them. Your fluffy chicken collection could be endless! Very fluffy, sort of fluffy, yellow and fluffy, not-so-fluffy…

Keep these ideas in mind as we build our model of behavior throughout the book.

What Is User Psychology?

Everything that can happen in a user's mind is important when they use your design. And a few things before that. And a few after.

Wait… let's back up for a second and talk about psychology in general

Just for a second.

Whether you're discussing dating psychology, or consumer psychology, or bathroom psychology, (which isn't so popular in grad school), you're still talking about the same brain we all got on our first day.

There is no special "user" part in there.

UX Design can affect that brain in lots of predictable ways. And that's what you're gonna learn: your brain, on design. All practical, all the time. No history, unless it matters. Nothing philosophical, because that's not how I roll. And no Sigmund Freud, because cocaine isn't considered a "best practice" anymore.

Just stuff you can use.

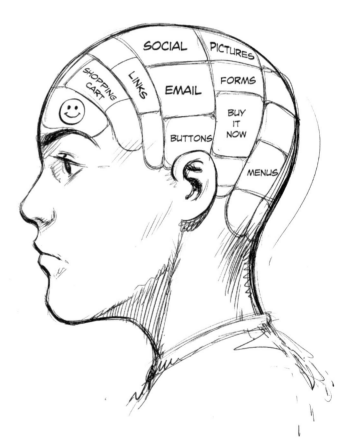

Why Do We Need User Psychology?

The answer: you can't be a great UX designer without psychology.

UX Design is the practice of creating nonrandom effects in people to solve a problem. In other words, you make them feel, think, and do stuff—on purpose. Therefore, the more you understand your users' feelings, thoughts, and actions, the better designer you are.

Understanding psychology allows you to answer things like why people share. Or why don't they choose the cheapest option every time? Or why does the design that got 200 Likes on Dribbble actually suck the big one?

(Yes, that's possible. Actually, it's pretty common.)

The answers might not be what you think! Your intuition lies to you all the time. (You'll learn about that in Lesson 33.) And sometimes the same design looks different to different people. You'll learn about that, too. And some things that seem super personal are actually universal human behavior. Guess what? You'll learn about that, too.

What Is An Experience?

There are probably many, endless conversations we could have about a philosophical "experience," but I am not qualified to teach you philosophy, so I won't. In UX, we need practical answers.

There are six big parts of an experience discussed throughout this book:

1. What the user *feels*

   In UX forums, this is what inexperienced designers talk about most. Making the user "happy." Asking them what they "like." Making users say "wow!" Users have feelings, and they are useful, but they are only a small fraction of an experience. The good things about feelings are that we can see them on a user's face, users can tell us about them, we can measure them, and we can relate to them, so feelings are easy to study.

2. What the user *wants*

   Much more important, but not as easy for the user to describe. A user's motivations are the engine of their behavior. Everything they do, click, choose, buy, and even what they see and hear depends on what they want. "When you're a hammer, everything looks like a nail." And if you change the way they see the situation, sometimes they will want something different.

3. What the user *thinks*

   It is helpful to imagine "thinking" as something the user carries, like bricks. Psychologists might call it *cognitive load*. Every time you make a user figure something out, or read more than a sentence of instructions, or learn a new feature, or hunt for the right link, or do two things at once, you're giving them another brick to carry. Most people can only carry a few bricks at a time. If you give them too many, they will drop everything.

4. What the user *believes*

Beliefs are tricky. The reasons people believe things are fairly predictable though. That's why you learned about psychology versus culture before this lesson. More important, your intuition has predictable flaws that most people don't know about. If you know about them— and you will—it allows you to predict what people will believe, before they believe it.

5. What the user *remembers*

Ironically, almost all designers forget about this one. Humans do not remember things like a video. Memories make mistakes. We only remember certain parts, we change those memories over time, and sometimes we remember things that never even happened! Your design can determine which parts someone remembers, and which are forgotten.

6. What the user *doesn't realize*

Ahhhh, yes. This separates good UX designers from other random people making wireframes. Most of our daily experience doesn't catch our attention. You have been breathing this whole time, but now you're aware of it. There's a low, constant noise all around you, but you weren't hearing it until right now. And that itch you just noticed… oh god… it's so itchy…

UX designers must also design things that users will never notice, never give you feedback on, and maybe never remember, like information architecture (which has a whole section in this book) and heuristics (models of how your users act). But that's a good thing! Unfortunately, though, no client will ever sit in a meeting and compliment you for it, (because they don't see it either). Those design elements will change the user's behavior, and only the data can show you how.

Conscious vs Subconscious Experience

In real life, your mind only puts attention on a small amount of the world around you. Otherwise you would be overwhelmed. This lesson is a basic idea with huge consequences.

Conscious Experience

You might hear UXers discussing something called "delight." Basically it is the art of designing something that makes a user say "wow!"

One thing must be true to create delight: the user must be aware of it, consciously. Daniel Kahneman, a Nobel Prize–winning psychologist, says our conscious mind is like "a *supporting character* who believes herself to be the lead actor and often has little idea of what's going on."

Sounds like Kanye West with the Kardashians, no?

Your conscious experience may feel like the whole experience, but it is actually just a small part. However, it's still significant. It is what makes people share, like, comment, download, and register. YouTube videos often explicitly tell you to subscribe at the end, because you may not consciously think of doing it otherwise.

Subconscious Experience

Subconscious experience seems like it "just is." It's how we decide what we trust, what we believe, and what is easy.

But there is never a moment when you "decided" to trust a website or an app. It just happened. And a user will only notice that your form design is easy if they expected it to be harder. Otherwise they might not even mention it. Things are *supposed* to be easy.

That is subconscious design.

If you want users to trust or understand, your design must feel trustworthy or obvious. If it doesn't, you can add as much delight as you want and it ain't gonna fix nothin'. Usability, for example, is the science of making your designs mentally invisible. You can see them, of course, but the more aware the user is of your form design, the worse the experience. It should feel automatic. The more clever you get with your form design, or your copywriting, the less people will finish the form.

Emotions

We have arrived at one of the core parts of psychology. The part that makes your pupils big or small, tears flow down your face, smiles happen, and more.

There is a lot of debate among *psychologists* about emotions. I'm gonna skip all that. This lesson is already a little longer than most, because emotions are super important in UX design. Instead—I give you the simplest practical model of emotions known to mankind:

- There are two categories of emotions: gain and loss.
- Emotions are reactions, not goals.
- Time makes emotions more complicated.

Gain and Loss

Emotions come in two flavors: good and bad; positive and negative; happy and unhappy. Pretty easy so far, right? I call them *gain* and *loss*.

Gains give you positive feelings. You might feel refreshed after a good night's sleep, or ecstatic after winning the lottery, or euphoric when your masseuse is a little more thorough than usual.

For now, just put them all in the same "happy" category.

Losses give you negative feelings. You feel grumpy when you haven't slept, or devastated after a breakup, or embarrassed when your masseuse turns out to be your cousin.

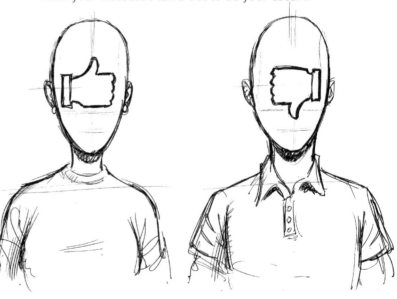

For now, just put them all in the same "unhappy" category.

Emotions Are Reactions, Not Goals

If I locked you in a dark box and gave you chemicals that would make you feel happy, forever, and then shot that box out into space, alone, with no communication, and you can't move or control anything, would you consider that a good thing?

Hmmm… maybe not. If you only make users "happy" it's like putting them in that box. Five minutes later, not so great.

There are two types of feelings: emotions and motivations. Motivations are what we want (goals), and emotions are how we feel when we gain or lose what we want (feedback). We'll learn about motivations next.

Time Makes Emotions More Complicated

Your emotions, or your "mood," change all the time. Within reason, that's normal. If it's extreme, you should probably see somebody about getting on reality television. But it's not all about here-and-now. You think in time. You remember the past and expect the future.

When you see a box wrapped in colorful paper, you think: gift! When someone says "we need to talk" you think: crap.

The "gift" might be full of snakes, but you will be happy until you know that. If you expect something bad to happen—like if the box is labeled "muthafuckin' snakes!"—you feel fear (or "worry" or "concern": if it's negative, it's negative). You will avoid it or try to escape. Unless you're on a muthafuckin' plane.

A more interesting emotion, in my opinion, is anger. If you want/expect something, but you can't get it, you will become aggressive toward whatever is stopping you. This is how emotions interact with time. When someone says "we need to talk" your first reaction is probably fear. You want to keep your job or your relationship, or whatever you think they are going to destroy. But when they actually do try to destroy it, you might get aggressive. Now they are stopping you from having it. When they succeed, you're sad (loss). If they change their mind, you're happy (gain).

What Are Motivations?

This lesson is about the most overlooked and the most powerful psychological element in UX: what users want.

The last lesson explained that emotions are reactions based on whether someone gains or loses their goals.

But what goals? *Motivations.* That's what.

Motivations are built-in psychological needs. Shit we want. Some are physical—you need them to survive—and some exist only in your mind. All are important. Motivations can fall anywhere between conscious experience and subconscious experience.

You can gain or lose each motivation, and you are motivated to do both. That will become very useful in UX, when you learn about conditioning.

Motivations are relative. That means it's not about how much you get, it's about how much more you get compared to what you have or what other people have.

In my book *The Composite Persuasion*, I outline 14 things that all people, everywhere, want. At least six of those motivations can be useful to you in (digital) UX and three of those are the foundation of gamification and social networks, like Facebook or Twitter. When you know how to use them, human motivations are UX magic in a bottle.

The 14 Universal Motivations

So, what are these 14 motivations?

Avoid death

Obviously, dying is bad. Evolution figured that out, too. You are motivated to live as long as possible (gain) and avoid anything life-threatening (loss), like heights, or fire, or snakes. Sometimes people commit suicide, but only when one of the other motivations is stronger than the will to live.

Avoid pain

Similar to death, but not necessarily life-threatening. This is ouchy pain like breaking your leg, not heartache pain like when 'N Sync broke up and left me with nothing. Nothing!

Air/water/food

Your body needs fuel to operate, and if it is running low, your motivations will make you fix that. The more urgent the need, the more desperate you get.

Homeostasis

This is your body's internal "balance." Remember the last time you drank too much, came home, went to sleep, and woke up an hour later to reverse-drink? That was your motivation for homeostasis. The same motivation also helped you pee during the evening and "detox" from the other end the next day. Try saying no to this motivation. I dare you.

Sleep

Recent studies have shown that sleeping might be your brain's cleaning and maintenance time. If you go long enough without sleep or if you watch C-Span for a couple minutes, your body and mind will take over and make sure you get some rest.

Sex

Sometimes called "seduction"—not to be confused with "romance," which is Love—this one is tricky, because it is counterintuitive. I will cover it individually in the next lesson.

Love

Also in the next lesson, Love comes in three different flavors, which give you a bad case of the feels for your family, your kids, and the person who lets you touch their fuzzy bits.

Protection of Children

You won't spend much time on this one, but it's good to know that it exists. Many things that involve adults have a different appropriateness or become more serious when they involve children. I am sure you can think of crimes that work like that. But sometimes, like with advertising, we just need extra rules and limitations to ensure safety. Why? Because in terms of evolution, people who can't reproduce yet are more valuable than those who have already, so we gotta protect 'em.

Affiliation

This is the motivation to belong to a group, and you will learn about it two lessons from now.

Status

This is the motivation to drive your own bus (metaphorically) and be better than others, and you will learn about it three lessons from now.

Justice

This is the motivation to balance the scales so everybody gets what they deserve; you'll learn about it four lessons from now.

Understanding (Curiosity)

The motivation to understand things is particularly interesting, and not as easy to use in UX as many people think. It will be your final lesson on motivations, and it will change how you think about usability, onboarding, advertising, and how users handle change.

This is a very brief introduction to motivations, but hopefully it gives you a sense of how UX can shape behavior. When users become loyal or have a deep appreciation for your product, it's because of *gains* in these motivations.

Motivation: Sex and Love

Ooooh, baby. Turn the lights down low. Light some candles and bring out those chocolate-covered strawberries, because it's time for a deeper look at two motivations that bring people closer together, online and offline.

Sex is the motivation to touch each other's warm and fuzzy parts, and love is the motivation that feels all warm and fuzzy. Here, we will learn about both, and they are surprisingly different.

But first, a bit of business…

Disclaimer

Sex can be a sensitive topic. First of all, it can be kind of shallow, so please don't be insulted. Second, there are certain political elements when talking about genders and behavior. I will use the terms "female" and "male" as categories, but let's be clear that the sexual behavior of a "male" doesn't always come with the body of a man, and vice versa. However, if I get too deep into the details, this lesson will get a bit hairy. Pun intended.

I ask, please, for the benefit of the doubt, and believe that everyone should be respected, regardless of orientation.

Sex Is About Reproduction

Females provide half of the process and males provide the other half, but those halves are distinctly different in a practical sense. Those differences cause a lot of our problems.

Think of sexual "rules of engagement" like an auction

If you have something valuable or rare, you want to give it to the person who can offer you the most, right? That's why *Antiques Roadshow* is so popular. The more valuable an item is, the more protective you should be, and the more people expect to offer for it. If you have a painting by Picasso, only the best bidders should show up. And, if you have a lot to offer, you only spend your time bidding on stuff like a Picasso.

On the other hand, if you don't have a lot to offer, then you look for the auctions that are a little less competitive. And, if you don't have something that is rare or valuable, then you might not have the same expectations. Sexual attraction is sort of like that.

It might *sound* simple enough when I use that analogy, but we're talking about people, so it is anything but simple. *Perception* is also a big part of it. It's not about how "valuable" or "rare" a person really is—because we are all unique snowflakes—it's about how valuable someone *seems*.

Some sexual signals are easy to see, like nice clothes or a fit body or a sign that says "Trust me, I'm Hot!" but others are much more subtle, like confidence and intelligence. And some signals are a matter of, ahem, personal taste. Like what you do for fun, or what music you like.

AS A UX DESIGNER

Provide the information users need to judge "quality" (popularity, interests, physical appearance, etc.) and to find whatever matches their taste. That can be as simple as a number of followers and a picture, or you might need videos and descriptions and niche categories.

This might sound absurd or surprising, but porn sites are actually some of the most active businesses when it comes to A/B testing and optimizing their designs, advertising, and search experience. It's an incredibly competitive industry, and they even have to consider one-handed navigation. Seriously!

We are also motivated to protect our chances of getting sex. A simple bit of text can create a lot of motivation, like: "Profiles with more photos are usually more popular." Once a user knows that, do you really think they will stick with one photo? More photos = better UX for everyone.

Love

If sex is shallow and short term, love is the opposite. It is made of hopes and dreams and caring and mutual interest and rainbows and sunshine.

Awwwwwww…

You can love a partner, or your kids, or your family, and those are all a little different. Love, basically, is the motivation to reciprocate motivations with someone else (i.e., you make them happy, and they make you happy).

With romantic love, the trick is finding someone who will love you back. We tend to pick spouses who share our values, (you agree about what is good/bad), so you need to design a way for users to find *themselves* in the crowd.

But where romantic love involves sex, loving your kids is more about protection and helping them grow, and loving family and friends is almost territorial. The features you design should help people behave like that.

AS A UX DESIGNER

Helping users find love is like helping them shop for a dishwasher. They only need one, and the basics are mostly standard, but everyone has their own idea of what is "perfect." Provide features to filter, compare, ask questions, save, follow-up, etc.

Motivation: Affiliation

Social media and games have become a huge part of the Internet, and the main motivations behind all of them are the same. One of those motivations is the desire to belong.

Affiliation, and the next two motivations, are purely relative. They only matter when you compare yourself to other people. My favorites.

Affiliation

Belong to a group. Any group. The fans of a team. People with "UX" in their job title. People from your home country. People who fish on the weekends. People who hate people who fish on weekends.

Whatever.

Being part of a group (or believing we are part of it) makes us feel proud. We wear their colors, sing their songs, buy their swag, display their symbols, etc. It could be a sports team, a band, a school, a country, or just your family. If your group has an opponent, there is a good chance you will hate that opponent. If your group has a common belief, there is a good chance you will hate anyone who disagrees with that belief.

AS A UX DESIGNER

Allow users to belong to a group or be identified by things they have in common—like joining guilds or "Liking" pages or choosing color schemes.

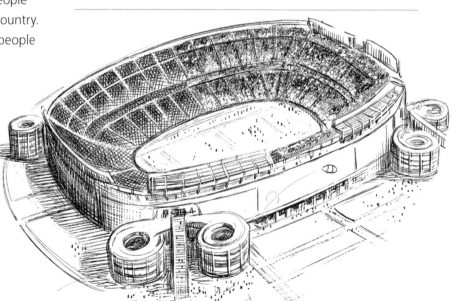

Motivation: Status

The other motivation that makes social networks and games work is the desire to control, compare, and compete with others to be the best.

Status

Decide for yourself. Call it freedom, or autonomy, or responsibility, or authority, or control, or rebellion. One way or another, you wanna be the boss, at least of yourself.

People always want to be in charge of themselves and their own decisions, even when someone else might do a better job, like when buying stocks or when that freedom might create more risk (like getting more responsibility at work).

You should let users have control, but help them make better decisions if you can and eliminate any chance of a major screw-up. Confirm dangerous choices or make those choices hard to do accidentally—"are you sure you want to launch the nukes, Mr. President?"

Be the best. Achievements, dominance, winning, popularity, money, talent, sex appeal, or some other version of that idea, which makes you more of something than most other people.

This is just straight-up competition, but it doesn't always come in the form of a game or a sport. Anything that can be done by all users, whether it is looking good in a profile picture or having the most followers, can (and will) become a competition. You just have to choose a way to use that competitive motivation.

Never move down. Remember: we are motivated to protect what we have gained. People will fight to keep their current status, even if it is made of something imaginary like points.

Sometimes adding a little bit of competitive risk is a good thing. If your farm will die while you're away, like in *Farmville*, or if your "activity level" will go down, like on Tumblr, then you will be more active to make sure you don't lose your status.

While I was writing this book, Instagram deleted millions of *fake followers* from the network—which was a good thing to do, for Instagram—and users got *upset* because their follower counts went down. They would rather have a bigger number of followers (higher status) that included robots than a lower number that was made of real people (lower status).

Motivation: Justice

Whether you think a kid deserves his black eye because he started the fight, or that the second kid is guilty for punching him, or that both kids were equally guilty, that's Justice.

Justice

The feeling that people should get what they deserve.

Everyone believes they deserve to be liked, even though most of us can be assholes from time to time. We all agree that Hitler was an "evil" leader rather than just a leader. And we all love to see underdogs win.

Justice is our emotional need for balance in the force.

The most interesting thing about Justice is that it only applies to the other motivations. If Person A has caused Person B to suffer a loss in one of the 13 motivations, we want Person A to suffer the same loss (or something equal). If Person A makes us happy by giving us gains in one of the other motivations, we feel like we owe them some recognition somehow.

On the other hand, if one kid beats up another kid, that might not seem fair to us as observers. But, if we then learn that he was fighting back against a bully, the feeling changes. If we find out the bully was falsely accused, it changes again. Morality is often a matter of perspective, which is probably why philosophers like to argue about it so much.

AS A UX DESIGNER

Have rules of conduct, or symbols of respect and honor, or give users the power to choose champions—like Twitter manners, Reddit Gold or Reddiquette, Kickstarter campaigns, or American Idol.

HOMEWORK!!!!!1!!!

Yes, homework!

Don't worry: your homework will be to stalk people on Twitter.

Go to Twitter. Try to find a profile description of a real person that does not name any group they are part of, any status they have achieved, or anything they morally believe or support.

(Blank profiles don't count, cheater.)

If you find one, let me know: @JoelMarsh.

Motivation: Understanding (Curiosity)

This is the motivation behind teaser trailers for new movies and your anger when Facebook suddenly changes their features without warning.

Understanding is the motivation to get information about a situation that involves the other 13 motivations. Sometimes we call it curiosity. We are also motivated to protect what we already understand. The funny thing about Understanding is that—even though it's pretty simple—designers and marketers screw it up all the time.

There are three rules for creating curiosity:

1. The user must understand enough to know there will be a gain or loss in one of the other 13 motivations.

2. The bigger the gain or loss seems to be, the more interesting it becomes.

3. Hold something back.

The illustration for this lesson is similar to the original iPhone's website. You see just enough to know that it's better than the not-so-smart phone in your pocket, but the specifics are hidden.

Voilá! You're curious.

If the iPhone looked like every other phone at the time, you wouldn't have felt curious, because you wouldn't "get it."

How to Screw It Up

The best way to suck at making people curious is to offer them something that isn't one of the other 13 motivations. Ironically, the most common example of this is a chance to *win an iPhone or iPad*.

First: everyone already understands an iPhone or an iPad. No curiosity.

Second: it's only a *chance* to win something that a lot of people already have (remember that Status is relative to other people.) So, the gain in Status is actually pretty small, unless you have no way to get an iPhone like if you're a kid, or you can't afford an iPhone, etc.

Instead, think of a way to make your product seem like a motivational gain, or not having your product seem like a loss. Stop trying to motivate people with a chance to get free shit.

AS A UX DESIGNER

You also have to consider the case when users *want* to understand, of course.

Users will choose something they understand over something they don't, if you give them a choice. It doesn't matter which one is actually better.

When you change or remove features, avoid using curiosity as a marketing strategy. Tell users what is coming, tell them why, show how it will work, and give them time to adjust, (if you can). Otherwise, users will be angry or afraid, because you're taking away something they already understand. That's a loss.

INTRODUCING IPHONE

IV

User Research

What Is User Research?

Ah, users. The sun in the UX solar system and the thorn in your side. One of the Sacred Laws of UX is "never blame the user," even though—let's be honest—sometimes it is really fucking tempting. However if you feel that way, you probably don't understand your users well enough. *Research is how we fix that.*

Different People Will Say That User Research Happens at Different Stages in the Process

Some say you should do it first. Some say you make some drawings and do it then. Some say you do it after building a working product.

They are all right. There is never a bad time to do user research. Do it early, do it often. The important question isn't *when*. It's *what*. As in "what are you trying to learn about your users?"

There are two main types of information that you can get from research that involves people: subjective and objective.

Subjective Research

The word "subjective" means that it is an opinion, or a memory, or your impression of something. The feeling it gives you. The expectations it creates. Not a fact.

"What is your favorite color?"

"Do you trust this company?"

"Does my ass look fat in these pants?"

(i.e., There is no right answer.) To get subjective information you have to ask people questions.

Objective Research

The word "objective" means a fact. Something true. Something you can prove. Your opinion doesn't change it, no matter how hard you wish.

"How long did you spend using our app?"

"Where did you find the link to our site?"

"What size are those pants?"

If people had perfect memories and never lied (especially to themselves), you could ask them about this stuff. If you find someone like that, let me know.

Objective data comes in the form of *measurements and statistics*. But, just because you can *count* something doesn't make it objective or "data."

> *The plural of "anecdote" is not "evidence."*
>
> —A wise person.

For example, if 102 people vote that something is good and 50 people vote that it's bad, the only objective information you have is the number of people that voted. Whether it is "good" or "bad" is still a subjective opinion.

With me so far?

(If not, I will blame myself for explaining badly, not you for reading badly.)

Sample Size

As a general rule, more people makes for more reliable information, even if it is subjective. One opinion could be completely wrong. If a million people agree, it is a good representation of the crowd's beliefs (but could still be false, objectively). So collect as much info as possible for your research.

Lots of subjective opinions can become... almost objective?! WTF

If you ask a crowd of people to guess the answer to something *objective*—like jelly beans in a jar—the average guess will often be pretty close to the real, objective, answer. But "wisdom of the crowd" about something subjective can also cause riots and get George W. Bush elected, so... yeah. Be careful. Subjective things can never be true; only more or less popular.

What Isn't User Research?

User research is very important and you should do it. But make sure you are asking users about what they think and feel, not what you should do next.

You Are Not Testing the Users; They Are Testing You

As the designer, you will be in a position of authority when you do user testing, but don't let it go to your head. The users are testing your design. If they don't do what you want them to do or if they don't understand, that's *your fault*, not theirs.

And if you lead them to the right answers by asking leading questions or giving them tips that normal users won't get, the test is ruined. You ain't proved nothin'. So when users are doing tests or giving answers, shut up and observe.

Users Are Not a Crystal Ball

UX is a set of skills, not a talent. Which means the average user can't help you do it, and it is a terrible choice if you're competing on *X-Factor*.

Therefore, your job is to listen to what the users say, not to be their design monkey. Listen to what users think, watch how they try to get things done, and understand how and why they get lost in your designs. Then go find solutions to those problems.

Don't ask users how they want their problems solved

If users think the button should be blue, or wish they could see all the products arranged by country of origin, or want you to smash little cymbals together and wear a cute little red hat, you can make note of it. But, if it doesn't help you achieve *your UX goals*, it probably isn't valuable right now. Ideas and solutions are different things.

Consensus Is Not a UX Strategy

Many designers think that a good way to find the best solution is to ask their colleagues. It's not. You should include colleagues in the design process to identify their requirements for the project and keep channels of communication open in general. That's what "working together" means.

But just because people at your company really love that button that makes a fart sound when you tap it—who doesn't?!—doesn't mean your users need it. And that includes you. You are a person at your company whose opinion doesn't matter. User research is *not* a way to confirm your beliefs; it's a way to discover them.

How Many Users Do You Need?

Should you go for the wisdom of the crowd, or should you trust your most loyal users? Should you ask the people who know the most about your designs, or the beginners who have fresh eyes?

This is a very common question, and a good one. How many users should you include in your user research to make sure that you get all the information you need? Well, it depends, actually.

The Less Obvious the Problem, the More People You Need to Find It

Let's say there are two problems with your design:

1. Most people don't notice the button that opens the menu.

2. Your pricing page makes it seem like your product is not free, but it is.

Both are real issues I have seen in testing.

Let's say the menu problem affects one out of every three people. That means you need *at least* three users to find the problem with the menu (it's more like four or five in real life).

And let's say the pricing problem affects 1 out of every 20 people. That means you need *at least* 20 users to find the problem with the menu (again, it's more like 30 or 40 in real life).

So if you get five test users—a common practice for user testing—you'll probably find the menu problem and *miss* the pricing problem. D'oh!

Since real services often only convert a few people out of 20 anyway, that pricing issue might be a significant amount of your sales! That is why face-to-face testing is useful, but not reliable in isolation.

Get Users Who Fit the Profile and A Couple Who Don't

In Lesson 29, *Creating User Profiles*, you will learn how to define the types of users who are important to you. By testing users who fit your profile in real life, you'll see how they think differently than you, and they will find problems that affect your real users.

BUT...

If you only test a single type of user, you'll miss any problems that are caused by other types of thinking. Throw in a few random weirdos—not your colleagues—just to see what they do. You might make some interesting discoveries.

How to Ask Questions

Often in UX—especially at the start of something new—you will need to ask real people some real questions, for realz.

Three Basic Types of Questions

The specific questions you ask will, of course, vary, but there are three basic types:

1. Open Questions—"How would you describe me?"

   This allows for a wide range of answers and works well when you want all the feedback you can get.

2. Leading Questions—"What are my best features?"

   This narrows the answers to a certain type. My example assumes that I have some good qualities, which might not be true. Be careful: this type of question also excludes answers you might want to know!

3. Closed/Direct Questions—"Which is better, my smile or my frown?"

   This type of question offers a choice: yes or no; this or that. But remember: if the options are stupid, the results will be stupid. Protip: don't be stupid.

Over the next few lessons you will look into some different types of research methods that involve questions of one type or another:

Observation

   Give people tasks or instructions and watch them use your design, without help. Afterward, you can ask them questions.

Interviews

   Get somebody and ask them a set of questions, one-by-one.

Focus Groups

   Get a bunch of people in a room together and ask them to discuss your questions.

> **NOTE**
>
> Confident people often persuade others in the group, and a few random people are an unreliable example of anything, which is why I would rather set myself on fire than do a focus group in real life.

Surveys

A form, which people answer on paper or online. These can genuinely feel anonymous, which is useful.

Card-Sorting

Each person gets a set of ideas or categories (on cards or post-its or online), which they sort into groups that make sense to them, personally. ProTip: don't use your colleagues for this.

Google

It's amazing how many useful opinions you can find online, for free, right now. Google is this website where you type in what you want and—oh, you've heard of it? Well, fine then.

Important

- Ask the same questions, the same way, to everyone.
- Avoid interpreting questions or suggesting answers.
- People might lie to avoid embarrassment or if it seems like you prefer a particular answer.
- Take notes or record the interview. Do not rely on your memory, ever.
- Don't eat yellow snow.

How to Observe a User

Watching someone is one thing. Observing a user for research purposes is a whole other thing. If you don't know the difference, you're probably doing it wrong.

Remember: Your Memory Sucks

Use video, take notes, have two people observing, or all of the above, because as my mom would say, "You can't trust your memory any farther than you can throw it." But that's a confusing metaphor in this case, so just make sure you record your research *as it's happening*. Don't rely on memory.

Read Between the Lines

Users often have body language or facial expressions or say, "hmmm…," or move their mouse in a way that reveals their thoughts and feelings during the test. If you have video of the screen and their face, you can take advantage of those real-time clues later.

Watch How They Choose, Not Just What They Choose

One of the most common mistakes for new UX designers is to ignore the process and only record the results.

The more the user *doesn't* do what you expect, the more useful the testing is. If you just end up with a page full of notes that say "complete" and "incomplete," you still know nothing. Instead, record how they navigate to the solution, why they think it is where it is, what clues they used to find it (or not), and whether *they* think they have completed the task or not.

Do Not Help

It will be very tempting to help a user who is confused or uncomfortable because they don't understand. Resist that temptation! The moment you help a user, or give them a hint, or point to something useful, the test is ruined because *you* are now testing the design instead of them. Letting users fail is sometimes the most useful result you can get.

True Story: People Will Lie to Get Your Approval

Don't forget that you are in the room. People will lie to cover embarrassment, or act helpless to get your help, or tell you the design is great when it isn't—just because you're sitting there.

Always approach user testing as if you expect users to lie about something, even if they don't realize it, because you can't trust a user any farther than you can throw them. There we go: best metaphor ever. Thanks, Mom!

Interviews

If you want to ask some questions or see people try something you have designed, you need to meet them face-to-face.

What Is an Interview?

An interview is a set of questions, created by you before the interview, asked to a user, in person.

Interviews are good because...

- You can ask follow-up questions; find out if your questions are confusing; give people tasks to complete; and get long, open answers to questions that might be harder to answer in writing.

- You can also watch users and get nonverbal clues, and you can learn about things where time limits are built into the experience, like games, quizzes, or real-time messaging.

- You can hand-pick the testers.

Interviews are bad because...

- You are there, so testers might adjust their behavior and opinions to get approval from you.

- It is harder to get real people to come to a place that is good for you, so you will usually end up testing with fewer users.

- The social nature of a face-to-face interview is not good for embarrassing or private products and services, like that site you buy all your latex body suits from.

- Introverted users probably can't imagine anything worse than a face-to-face interview.

You should do interviews when...

You need to test subjective stuff with many steps or decisions involved, like navigating around a site to select the perfect latex body suit. Or if you need to ask follow up questions depending on the user's behavior, like "which ball-gag goes with that body suit, in your opinion?"

Surveys

Face-to-face interviews aren't always an option, so sometimes you need to send questions out to people. But be careful, there are things a survey can do, and things it can't.

What Is a Survey?

A survey is a set of questions that a user answers by filling out a form on paper or online, privately, and sometimes anonymously. It's like a Buzzfeed quiz, but instead of finding out which Harry Potter character you are, you just give feedback.

Surveys are good because...

- They allow users to participate privately and therefore be more honest.

- Every user gets precisely the same questions, and you (the designer) can't screw it up by asking the questions wrong.

- It is easy and cheap to get thousands of people to answer a survey. If you do that in person then you also need portable toilets, food trucks, bands to perform... it's a hassle.

- Nobody has to feel disappointed, because a UX survey never says you are most like Malfoy.

Surveys are bad because...

- You can't ask follow-up questions, so it takes more careful preparation to create a survey.

- It's easy to accidentally influence the results by how you ask the question or the order you choose for the options.

- People are lazy, so the longer you make the survey, the fewer people will complete it.

- You can't retake a survey to choose all the answers that make you Harry or Hermione, even if you know—in your heart—that you're not like Malfoy.

You should use surveys when...

You want to compare the answers of users to each other, or control the way questions are asked, or ask a lot of people, or control the mix of ages, genders, locations, etc.

Card Sorting

Some types of questions are hard to answer, so it might be better to get a user to show you instead.

What Is Card Sorting?

Not a way to win Blackjack more often. Unfortunately.

Basically, you give each user a set of topics or ideas written on "cards"—maybe types of content or features you're considering—and ask them to organize the cards into categories that make sense to the user.

Card sorting can literally be a bunch of recipe cards, or you can use an online tool to simulate it. By doing this with many users and then documenting the relationships they create between cards, you will learn which ideas or features are most related in the minds of the users, and it will help you design menus and information architecture. It sounds a bit complex, but I have done this with a whole class of students in 15 minutes, during the class, using online tools. It

took about an hour to create cards for an agency's future site content—before the students arrived—and the students were able to sort them quickly while I ignored them completely, like the amazing teacher that I am. The software did all the work of measuring the patterns in their choices and probably saved me hours of work. Voilá!

Card sorting is good because...

- Designing big, complex sites like Wal-Mart or eBay can seem overwhelming at the beginning. Card sorting helps you get started.

- You can discover structure within a pile of ideas that seem random or unrelated, or learn about the priorities of your audience without asking them directly.

- I did card sorting for a digital agency's website, because I understood the content *too well* and couldn't think about it from the users' perspective. It also revealed differences in the way clients and prospective employees thought about the agency.

Card sorting is bad because...

- It is definitely a bit tedious to set it up, and the answers are more of a guide than a solution.

- Card sorting is only as good as the material you put into the experiment.

- Users will organize the cards you provide for them, whether that makes sense or not.

- If your site/app is a tool, like email, or something less traditional, like Tinder, card sorting might give you unhelpful results. Card sorting is designed to reveal assumptions and expectations, not innovation.

Use card sorting when...

You know what types of content or features you want to include, but the actual strategy for organizing that content isn't so obvious.

Creating User Profiles

Just like marketers have a target audience, UX designers have user profiles or personas: descriptions of users, based on research.

What a Profile Is Not

First of all, let's nail down what personas or profiles are *not*:

- Personality types
- Demographics
- Characters in your "brand story"
- Stereotypes based on your experience
- Shallow or one-dimensional
- Concepts
- Predictions

So, What Is a User Profile/Persona?

Profiles or personas describe the goals, expectations, motivations, and behavior of real people. Why do they come to your site? What are they looking for? What makes them nervous? And so on. All the information you need should be in your research and data. If you can't back it up with research or data, you're just making shit up and you should stop.

Bad profile

Persona A is a male, between the ages of 35 and 45 with an above average income and education. They have at least one child and own at least one new vehicle. They are outgoing and career-oriented, and tend to be right-brain thinkers.

Why it's bad

That might be great if you're selling ads, but as far as UX goes, that profile is basically useless. Why? Because it doesn't allow you to say "no" to any feature ideas. What sort of features does a male between 35 and 45 need? It could be anything!

Useful profile

Persona A is an experienced manager, mostly interested in one or two areas of expertise. They visit often, but they are pressed for time, so they focus on "collecting" content to read on the weekends. They tend to be prolific social-media sharers, mostly to Twitter and LinkedIn. They consider themselves thought-leaders, so public image is important.

Why it's useful

Now you have a lot of information to use! You know that fluffy content will not be popular, self-curating will be a big deal and you have a basis for setting up content categories. They need easy access to sharing, and only certain types of social sharing will be relevant.

You also get to say "no" to a Facebook campaign, because these users don't spend time there, and "digest" emails (a summary of weekly activity) will be better than frequent notifications because these people are already pressed for time.

Think of "Ideal" Users; Several of Them!

When you think about features, think of the most valuable version of the users you see in real life. You're not trying to support the current behavior; you're

trying to nudge those users toward an "ideal" version of themselves.

Also remember that all users are not alike! You will probably have a few different behavioral groups, and they all deserve a good profile.

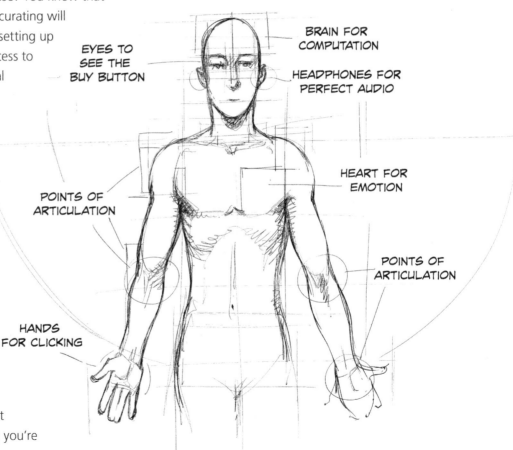

EYES TO SEE THE BUY BUTTON

BRAIN FOR COMPUTATION

HEADPHONES FOR PERFECT AUDIO

HEART FOR EMOTION

POINTS OF ARTICULATION

POINTS OF ARTICULATION

HANDS FOR CLICKING

Devices

In today's world, we're not just talking about a single phone or laptop. Follow these six steps to help you think about designing for different devices:

Step 1: Finger or mouse?

I am not going to cover this here, because Lesson 69, *Touch versus Mouse* is completely dedicated to this idea.

Step 2: Start small.

Many people think "mobile first" has something to do with mobile being popular. Kind of, but not really: if you design for the smallest, least powerful device first, then you will focus on the content and your core functionality. That leads to simple, beautiful apps/sites. If you do it the other way around, it'll be like trying to put a marshmallow into a piggy bank, which is neither simple, nor beautiful.

Step 3: What special powers does this device have?

Mobile devices travel with us so—surprise!—we spend more time on them and location becomes a factor. They are also small, so moving the device itself can be a feature. Laptops, on the other hand, don't travel as well, but they are more powerful, they have huge screens and keyboards, and the mouse allows more precise selections and functions. Don't worry about "consistency" so much—different devices require different thinking sometimes.

Step 4: Consider the software.

"Mac versus PC" is more than a cute ad campaign. Read through the UX guidelines before you start. Also, iOS 7 or Windows 8 look different than iOS 6 or Windows Vista. You might need to choose which versions you will support and which you will ignore. Every time you support one, it multiplies the design, development, and maintenance time in the future. Think ahead!

Step 5: Be responsive.

Is it on the Web? Does it support a few different types of phones? What if Apple makes a new iPhone that is a little different? The modern Internet—whether it is a website or an app—works on all devices. Decide whether a couple different layouts will do the job or whether you should create a fully responsive site for all types of customers.

Step 6: Think about more than one screen at a time.

This one is a bit advanced, but I think you're ready for it. Can you use your phone and computer together, like a remote and a TV? Could a group of phones control a game on a tablet, all in the same room? What if you're logged in on two devices, can you "throw" data from one to the other? Can the location of one device be used on another? What about syncing information; will that cause issues in real-time? What if two users log in to the same account at the same time, on different devices? Give it some thought!

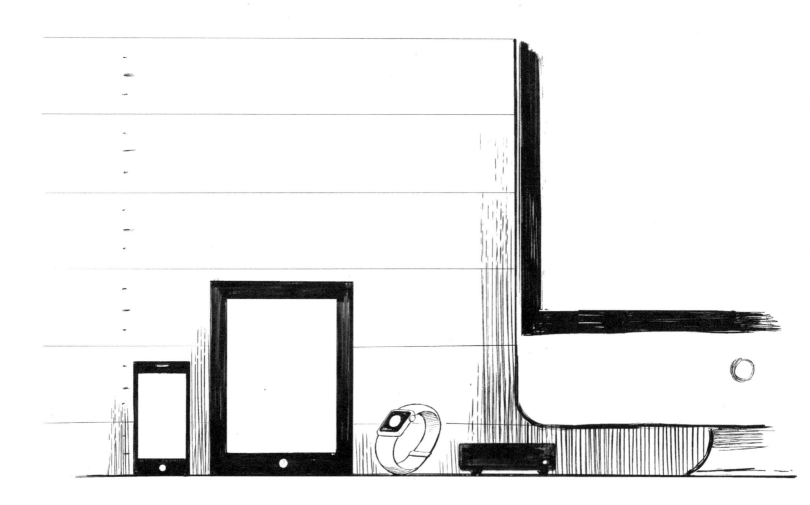

V

The Limits of Our Minds

What Is Intuition?

One word you will hear fairly often in UX design is "intuitive." That means the user will understand without much explanation or training. *Not you.*

Intuition is often called common sense. Or, your "gut feeling." And some people believe they have a special talent for intuition (nope). But, for everyone, your intuition always feels true. However, common sense isn't as common as you might think. Intuition is *not* something you are born with. Trust me, babies make terrible UX designers. Intuition is constructed from your experiences; you expect certain things based on what you have experienced before.

People from North America might be confused when they go to a public toilet in Asia and only see a hole in the floor. Whereas two people from Asia might be equally confused about squatting over those crazy water chairs in North America.

Intuitive, schmintuitive. Normal is relative.

The tricky part for many people is that your beloved intuition can also be wrong when there is a right answer. Really, really often.

As a UX Designer, Gut Feelings Can Be Your Worst Enemy

You will often hear people say "trust your gut." That is stupid advice, because everybody trusts their gut. You're born that way. It's like saying "eat what tastes good." I might not be a doctor, but that isn't the best advice if you want to be healthy. (We will learn why it still

feels like good advice, in the next lesson, *What Is a Cognitive Bias?*)

Trusting your gut guarantees you will be wrong eventually. Many times. Not trusting your gut is the only way to avoid those mistakes.

A UX Designer's Job Is to Design for *Other People's* Gut Feelings

Not your own.

When it comes to thousands or millions of users, "intuitive" means that most people understand it, regardless of whether you are included in "most people."

You know too much, remember?!

Saying your own design is intuitive is like saying you are the smartest person in the mirror. You need data and user feedback to know for sure. That's how I *know* that I am the smartest person in my mirror.

What Is a Cognitive Bias?

Your brain is a system. Certain types of information go in, certain types of decisions come out. But like many systems, if you give it information it wasn't designed for, you can get less-than-perfect results.

Have you ever seen *The Matrix*? When Neo (Keanu Reeves) meets The Architect, it is revealed that there have been other Neos before. They are a "systemic anomaly" that happens from time to time. A flaw in the system.

Cognitive biases are sort of like that. If you ask people certain types of questions, or ask in a certain way, the "intuition system" will reliably choose the wrong answer. Those "mistakes" are something we can use in UX design. We can let users choose whatever they want, and most of the time they will choose what we want. If you do it right.

Some examples will help:

Anchoring

The first number you say affects the next number in someone's head. For example, if you ask people to donate to a charity, they might give an average of $2. But if you "suggest" a donation of $10, the average will go up to something more like $5. Nothing changed, but you anchored donors to $10, which made $2 feel lower.

Next time you want a raise at work, aim high. You won't get the full amount, but the raise you get will be higher than it would have been otherwise.

Bandwagon Effect

The more people who believe something, the more likely it is that other people will believe it, too. Information doesn't become more true or more false because lots of people believe it, but your brain doesn't know that. Your mom always said, "If everybody jumped off a bridge, would you do it, too?" (Because all the other moms say that.)

This is why you should usually show how many people have Liked, registered for, or shared something. It's also why informercials say garbage like "a million people can't be wrong!"

Oh yes they can!

Decoy Effect

This is one of my favorites. Imagine you want to subscribe to a newspaper, and these are the choices:

- Web Only: $10

- Print Only: $25

- Print & Web: $25

Which one is the best deal? After a few seconds to consider it, there is about an 80% chance that you think Print & Web is the best value.

Why? Because the Print Only price is the "decoy"—nobody will choose it. Its only purpose is to make the most expensive price look like a good deal. Even though nobody chooses it, if you remove it, about 60% of people will choose the cheapest option instead.

It's not rational. *It's biased.* If you have an election coming up soon in your country, think carefully.

There are *many types of cognitive biases*; too many for this course.

The Illusion of Choice

Regardless of what you are designing, it's only a matter of time before you have to let your users choose their own adventure. Whether it's a menu, a set of prices, or a list of products, UX affects that choice.

Many new designers think about user choices as a random event. The users could pick anything!

Well, sort of.

They can choose randomly, but they won't. And they shouldn't. Sometimes, it really doesn't matter (to us) what the user chooses. But sometimes it is the difference between success and failure. Always give users the options they need, and make sure everything is easy to find, but—as a UX designer—you can also maximize your own goals, without sacrificing anything for the user.

Here are four good principles:

1. The Paradox of Choice

   In theory, choosing *nothing* is always an option.

   The more options you offer someone, the harder it is to choose. That's called the Paradox of Choice. If the user can't decide, they will leave. Providing lots of options might feel like "something for everyone," but you're

actually giving every user a small aneurysm. Choosing carefully from three things is easy. Choosing carefully from 30 things is impossible.

2. What You See Is All There Is

   Most people will only consider the choices that they are offered, even if other possibilities exist. On the TV show *The Bachelor*, you never hear him say, "The second rose goes to... the camera guy, Bruce."

   Bruce might deserve that rose, but he's not an option. If The Bachelor could still choose from everyone on Planet Earth, it wouldn't be a good show. Whether you're designing shipping options, or subscription features, or survey questions, this is important. Every choice should take the user closer to their goal, and you can design the choices so they are good for your goals in the process.

3. Choose Defaults Wisely

Dan Ariely's Ted Talk about decision-making includes one of the best examples of good/bad defaults that I have seen.

In a nutshell: countries that made people *choose* to be an organ donor got very few people to do it. Countries that made people choose *not* to be an organ donor had more than 90% organ donors.

It's easier for a user do nothing than to do something. The lazy option should be the best one for your company and—ideally—for the user. If the user can truly choose "anything"—like a pay-what-you-want situation—then anchoring is the way to set a default in their mind.

4. Comparisons Are Everything

Users are choosing things based on comparing their options. Therefore, you should create comparisons that make your preferred options look better. In the previous lesson, we learned about the *Decoy Effect*. That's one way to make an option look better. Here are some more:

- You can point out which option is the "best value," or the "most popular," or "most edible."

- You can present subscriptions as "per month" or "per day" prices so users can see that yearly subscriptions are cheaper per month, even though they are more expensive in total.

- Describe which type of people should choose each option. Which one is more *you*? Many products have a "pro" version so it comes with some status. Are you an amateur or a pro?

- Put your features in a list so the user can see what they "lose" by choosing the free version instead of the premium version.

- Have a sale! Forever! Include the "regular" price so users can see how much they are "saving." Make sure they save the most on the most profitable option.

I could go on, but you get the idea.

Attention

This lesson is about one simple idea that most people think about in the wrong way. However, that one idea can affect everything in your approach to design.

Your brain can only consciously do one thing at a time, so it has to focus. That focus moves from one thing to another, all day long. That's called *attention*. Ironically, most designers forget about attention. It seems so simple, yet we constantly overlook it. From what I have seen, people treat attention like a ticking time bomb. They do as much as possible, hoping that something will create interest, before time runs out.

That's not how attention works.

Attention is like a spotlight. It points at a specific thing. If you want to point it at something else, you have to stop pointing it at the first thing. As you move the spotlight, anything outside of the light will go unnoticed. The other columns of content. The banners. The other banners. And the custom banners that you call something else internally so it doesn't feel like you're advertising to your own users (still banners!).

If you want people to notice something, it either has to be close to the spotlight or obvious in the dark.

"Whoa."—Ted "Theodore" Logan

Here are a few ways to get the attention of users:

Motion

This is the highest-ranking part of your visual system, so when something moves, your attention is drawn to it by reflex. But if everything is moving, the stationary item gets the attention.

Surprise

This is not the same thing as "shock" or "delight"—this is the principle behind pattern breaking in Lesson 54. When something doesn't match what we expect, we notice.

Big text

This usually indicates the "main information" in the design, so our eyes tend to go there first.

Sound

Audible alerts can be one of the most annoying things on the Internet, but it does get your attention. When used more elegantly, it works well.

Contrast and Color

These can make parts of your design jump out from your peripheral vision. Users will notice those parts without looking directly at them. This is covered in Lessons 52 and 53.

What Are You Sacrificing to Get Attention?

Every time you add an extra message or pull someone's attention with motion or sound, you are also stealing their attention from everything else. "Paying" attention really does have a "cost": an *opportunity cost*.

It might be fun when people comment on that all-singing, all-dancing User Interface (UI) detail somebody worked so hard on, but if that causes them to miss the Buy Button, it's a bad design choice. If a UX designer wants to design "everything a user can experience," she's missing the point of attention.

UX isn't about creating a perfect world. It's about eliminating everything that competes with our goals and user goals. Good UX is *reductive, not expansive*.

If God were a UX designer, you would be sitting in a small, dark, sound-proof room, in a comfortable chair, with no clock, using a device that could only display his website or app.

Who knows, maybe you are.

"Whoa."—Bill S. Preston, Esq.

Memory

The experiences you remember are not complete, accurate, honest, and sometimes they aren't even real. That means it is possible to "design" what people remember.

Memory Is Really Cool

This lesson barely scratches the surface.

You base a lot of decisions on your memories, but your long-term memories might be different than they appear. Our brains *don't record memories like a video*. Memories are reconstructed, from associations, each time you think about them. But associations change over time. You might become an expert in physics, or grow out of your go-to-school-dressed-like-a-vampire phase.

That means it will become impossible for you to remember physics like a beginner, or to think about fake fangs as a cool accessory. Each time you remember something, you change that memory forever.

All Memories Are Not Created Equal

Your brain puts more emphasis on the experiences that have stronger feelings and more "novelty" (they grabbed your attention, at the time). Your brain is also good at remembering patterns and things you do over and over. That's called practice, or a *habit*, or muscle memory.

AS A UX DESIGNER

You should read those last few sentences as tools that you can use in your designs. Part of that is done by using all the skills you have learned so far. Part of that is done after the experience is over.

Emphasize with Bias

In my book *The Composite Persuasion*, I dedicated a whole chapter to the idea of changing people's memories. Here are a few tips:

Remind them of the good parts.

If you buy a Macbook from Apple, the next email you get will be full of feature highlights. I'll bet you a high-five that it changes the way you remember your reasons for buying.

Create habits.

It is useful to build patterns of clicks/touches that people can learn and repeat quickly. Think: Tinder swipes. It might be new at the beginning, but once users can do it easily, they will remember it as being obvious the whole time. (Photoshop, anyone?)

Personalize.

Many websites use your choices to improve your next visit. My Pinterest feed is about 80% things I like now, but my first experience was only about 10% things I liked. Same with Reddit. However, I just know that. I don't remember it.

Research and Memory

Nothing a user says in an interview or on a survey should be considered a fact. It is merely an impression. I once saw a survey where users were asked, "What website did you visit before this one?" The Google Analytics data showed that more than 30% of people were wrong, and that was a memory from five minutes before.

Your memory is the same. You should record interviews or take notes that are good enough for someone else to use, and document your research (with sources!).

Beware of False Memory

Believe it or not, some things we remember are completely false. They never happened, and they are not a version of a real event. There are videos on YouTube of people experiencing false memories in real life.

Still want to do everything users say?

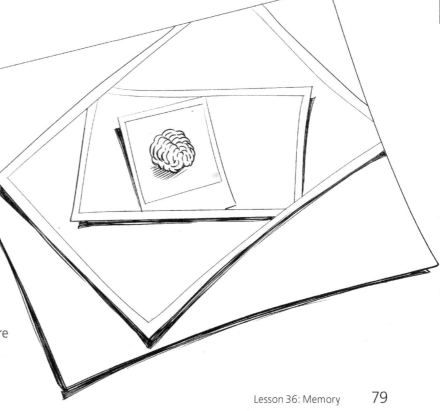

Hyperbolic Discounting

Usability is a big area of the UX world, and it is a critical element in most—if not all—projects. There is one cognitive bias that forms the backbone of usability, and it affects the way we predict the future and ourselves.

Hyperbolic Discounting might sound like a complex piece of mathematics, but it is actually a fairly simple idea:

> *Whatever is happening to you now (or soon) seems more important than what will happen to you later (or in the future).*

It applies to your perception of value, and how you judge your own emotions, and how you make important decisions. It's why most people don't save money well, and why plans almost always take longer than expected. People get fat because eating unhealthy food is easier and more fun "now" than working out to be fit "later."

Usability is basically the idea of getting people to the things they want as close to "now" or with as little effort as possible. The more work it takes or the longer they have to wait, the worse the experience *feels*.

Motivations versus Time

Earlier, in Lesson 15, you learned how time affects emotions, but not how it affects motivations. Check it out:

Imagine that I offer you $100 now, or $120 next year. In real life, you would probably take $100 now, even though $120 is clearly more money. Now imagine you want something that costs $100 now, or $50 next year, or $10 per month over the next 12 months.

In real life, most people will pay $10 per month—like you did with your smart phone—because it is the best option "now." Even though that is the most expensive option later (do the math!).

Usability Is a Two-Way Street

In UX, we talk about usability a lot. Most of the time we want things to be easier, faster, simpler. Those are things the user wants now. Everything in your design should be based on getting users to the most valuable actions as quickly and easily as possible. But your design should also make destructive actions more time consuming and unemotional so they feel less appealing.

Like Facebook does.

When you try to deactivate your Facebook account, it uses Hyperbolic Discounting to change your mind. The form is long and boring, so your emotions have time to decrease. Near the end, it shows you pictures of friends you will lose now, which replaces the impulsive motivation to destroy Facebook (and everything associated with it) later.

Most people quit before deactivating, even though, technically, nothing is stopping them.

VI

Information Architecture

What Is Information Architecture?

So far, we have mostly discussed the ways to understand users and UX. In this lesson, we actually start making shit. The first step in designing a real solution is the general structure of the thing.

Information Architecture (IA) is the idea of giving a bunch of information some structure (i.e., organizing it, somehow). IA can be relatively simple with a small project, and incredibly complicated with a large project. IA is invisible. To work with it, we need to draw a *site map*.

This example shows a website with six pages: The home page, two sections in the main menu, and three subsections. The lines indicate which pages are connected by navigation (menus and buttons).

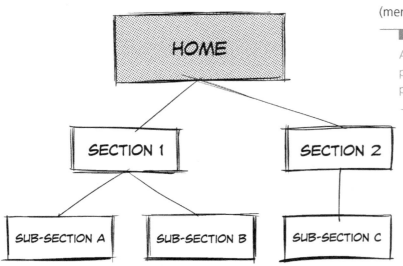

> **NOTE**
>
> A million users doesn't mean you have a million profile pages. You have one profile page that can display any user's profile.

When pages are organized this way—like a family tree—it is called a "hierarchy" or "tree." Most sites and apps are organized like this (but it's not the only way).

There are no "rules" for drawing site maps, but here are some general guidelines:

- Just because it looks simple, doesn't mean it makes sense.
- Keep it clear and readable.
- We usually draw top-to-bottom, not left-to-right.
- Don't make a site map "fancy." It's a technical document, not a fashion show.

Deep or Flat, Not Both

Generally speaking, your site map will either be very "flat"—which includes more sections in the menu and requires fewer clicks to reach the bottom—or your site map will be "deep"—simpler menus, but more clicks to get where you're going.

Notice that both of the structures in this example have the same number of pages. Equal, but different.

Sites with a lot of products, like Wal-Mart, often need a deep architecture; otherwise, the menus get ridiculous. Sites like YouTube, which only has users and videos to deal with, are usually more flat. If your site is deep *and* flat, that's bad. You might want to simplify your goals, or design a good search as a core feature.

COMMON MYTH

You might hear people say that everything should be "three clicks away" at all times. This means they learned UX in the '90s and haven't learned anything new since then. Focus on the user instead. Make sure they understand where they are and where they can go, at all times. If your navigation is easy and clear, the number of clicks is irrelevant.

FLAT:

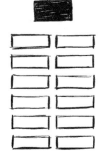

DEEP:

User Stories

Information Architecture is not always easy to explain. It helps if you can talk about it with your team and think about it easily in your own head. *User stories* help you do that.

A user story describes one possible path a user can take in your site or app. It should be short, but complete. You will need many user stories to describe your whole design.

A basic user story for Google.com might look like this:

1. The user arrives on the main search page.

2. The user can enter any search query and submit it with the mouse or keyboard.

3. The next page displays a list of search results with the most relevant results on top.

4. The user can click a link to go to the appropriate site, or they can navigate through more pages of results until they find something useful.

This is a little too simple, but you get the idea.

Notice that nothing in the story tells me specifically how to solve or design those actions, just that they are possible. The purpose of these stories is to describe flows. Sequences of user choices. Not the final UI.

If the flows are simple and effective, you are doing a good job (so far).

Managers often think user stories are a way to order UX from the designer, but that is absolutely wrong. Why? Because a user story is basically a list of features or functions, and that has a major effect on the final solution. The UX Designer writes user stories to communicate to the team, *not the other way around.* That would be like telling *Bob Ross* what colors to use! (I was gonna say Michelangelo there, but let's be honest, I made the right choice.)

Types of Information Architecture

There are many ways to organize a bunch of information. Depending on the type of content or the goals of your project, different structures can be better or worse.

Ok, so now that you can write user stories, we need to bring your IA back into this. The structure of your pages determines the steps in your user stories. And to structure your pages, you have to pick a type of IA to work with (or a couple types, but let's keep it simple for now).

Types of IA include:

- Categories
- Tasks
- Search
- Time
- People

Let me break it down for you (cue the DJ):

Categories

When you think of a retail store like H&M, you probably imagine its menu as a set of categories: "Men, Women, Kids, Sale," and so on. Types of content. When you click those categories, you expect to see content that fits in that category.

This is the most common type of IA. However, if the categories are complex, like banking products, industrial chemicals, or sex toys (a friend told me), then you and your users might not have the same expectations about what is in those categories, and that can get confusing. If I want to buy a butt plug, is that under "Battery-Operated" or "Glow-in-the-Dark"? Life is full of hard questions.

Tasks

Another way to organize your site or app is by the goals the users need to achieve. If you are a bank, perhaps something like "Save, Loan, Invest, Get Help, Open an Account" would make a simpler menu. If the user knows what they want, this is a great way to structure your design. But be careful: users don't always know enough to choose their own adventure.

If you think about it, you will realize that a task-based site and a category-based site for the same company could look very different. It's an important choice.

Search

If your site is very complex, or if it is mostly full of user-generated content, a search-based architecture like YouTube might make more sense. If YouTube only had categories (Funny, Sad, Ads, Movies, etc.) it would actually be hard to use and require a lot of work to keep the categories correct!

Time

If you're just starting in UX, this might blow your mind a little: you can also design IA that changes with time. The simplest version would be your inbox, where messages are displayed in the order they arrived. That is *time-based* IA design. On a site, you would have pages for things like "hot right now, archived, later, new," etc. Reddit or the Facebook News Feed are also examples of time-based design.

People

Facebook—or any social network—is IA based on people. All of the pages are designed around who the information is about, and the relationships between them. Once you are on someone's profile, Facebook uses categories (Photos, Friends, Places) to organize different types of content.

And there are probably many other types!

Static and Dynamic Pages

Some pages are always the same. Some pages are different for every user. Two different types of layout means two different types of design thinking.

What Is a Static Page?

A static page (or screen) is the most basic form of a digital layout. It will look precisely the same every time, for every user. It is *hardcoded*.

A real-life example might be that website you made when you were 13 that had a bunch of random animated GIFs in a chaotic layout beside a photo of your celebrity role-model and a slightly-too-honest-yet-vaguely-intriguing introduction of your super mature 13-year-old self.

Or, you know, images in your portfolio.

But static pages aren't worse. They're just simpler. Many product pages on *apple.com* have been static, because they were just pictures and text. Why over-complicate it?

What Is a Dynamic Page?

A dynamic page is a page that isn't always the same. It changes. For example:

- A dynamic page might *react* to your choices. When you choose more expensive shipping during the checkout flow, the total price changes automatically without leaving the page.

- A dynamic page might look different depending on the user. Every person's Facebook profile can show different content in the same page design because the page is *dynamic*.

- A dynamic page might act as a template for lots of content. Every article on the *New York Times* site might use the same page as a template, but the page fills itself with the article you have chosen each time.

Things versus Containers

Static design is more about the *exact* layout, because static design doesn't "do" very much. The things you design just sort of… sit there… like a boss!

For dynamic pages you have to design *containers*, not the content itself. You can never be *exact*.

A space for *any* headline. A space for *any* product image. A space for 15,000 posts about anything from babies, to Bieber, to latté art, to Bieber as a baby, to Bieber as latté art, and so on.

Containers can be different heights (short article or long article), different widths (short headline or a long headline), or they might even be empty sometimes!

Create No-Fail Scenarios

If a really long headline will break your layout, change the layout or don't allow people to make headlines that long. If your layout will completely go to hell because somebody posted a tiny little photo, change the layout, or don't allow them to upload tiny little photos.

Usually, it's better if you change the layout. But don't be afraid to create useful limitations so users will make more effective choices. 140 characters didn't hurt Twitter, right? Just don't be that designer who puts unnecessary limits on users because "This is the way the layout should be." Users don't like that guy.

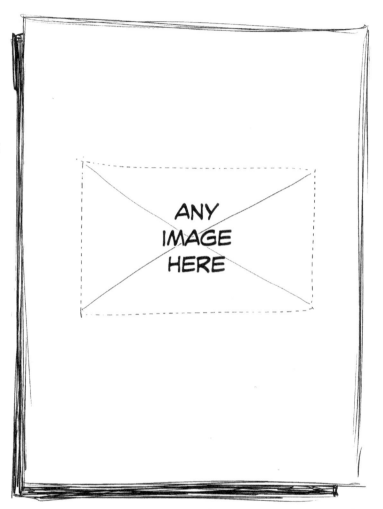

What Is a Flow?

If you want users to get from A to B, you have to design how they get there. And you definitely want users to get from A to B.

Imagine your users as a crowd of people in a physical place, like Grand Central Station in New York City. There are several predictable ways the crowds will move around the station, and if you're the architect designing the station, you have to make sure the crowd moves easily.

An app or a website is a similar concept. Thousands or millions of people need to move through your Information Architecture without getting stuck or lost, and the easier it is for them to "flow" to where they want to go, the better your design will perform and the happier the users will be.

Whether they are flowing through the checkout, through projects in your portfolio, or through the registration process on Facebook, this is important to think about.

Just like most people will go from the front door to a train, or from one train to another, your app or site will have common paths to consider, too.

Don't Count Clicks or Pages

The architect of Grand Central Station didn't count how many steps people would take or how many doorways they would go through, because it doesn't matter.

It is more important to give people the right information at the right time so they know whether to turn left or right to find their train. A long hallway, like a flow with many pages, can be very simple to use, even though it's long. And a short hallway with too many signs can be confusing, like a website with complex menus, even though it is "only" one choice.

Avoid Making a "Dead End"

If you send a crowd of people into a hallway with no exit, you're going to have problems, especially if someone farts.

If users navigate through several pages only to arrive at a page with no "next step," they will leave or get lost, or get angry. Make sure there is always somewhere to go, and make sure the users know how to get there.

Users Don't Go Backward

It is really common to imagine your users navigating back to the page where they started or using the back button to find what they need. It is also really wrong.

User Motivation Is Rare, Not Common

When most people imagine users using their design, they imagine them reading all the text and checking every menu item and navigating right to the bottom of the site to find what they need.

If a user were being held hostage and had to explore your site under threat of waterboarding, they still might not be that thorough. If the user isn't finding what they want, every extra click a user makes increases the odds that they will leave your site.

That includes clicks on the back button.

Users Only Go Backward When Confused or Lost—That's Bad

You might think of your site as a tree with several branches, but users only think about the navigation options they can see right now or those that they have already used.

If a user clicks the back button, it doesn't mean they are going "up a level" to retry their last decision. It means they have no fucking idea what to do. In a user's mind, the back button is the "abort" button or the "nope" button. If, during user tests, you see users hitting "back" a lot, it means they are not finding what they want. And since you are probably sitting there watching them, it probably means that they would leave the site when they are alone.

Make Loops If You Want Users to Go Backward

When I say a "loop," I mean something like this:

- Page A links to Page B.
- Page B links to Page C.
- Page C links to Page A.

The user can keep clicking forever without leaving your site.

Let's say this loop is your portfolio site. Page A shows the categories of work you have done. Page B is a list of projects within one category. Page C is details about one project. The user can pick a category, then a project, then read the details, and then navigate back to the categories without ever using the back button to navigate. They could see your entire portfolio without ever going "backward."

If users can always click *forward*, they never have to stop and *decide* where to go next. Decisions are hard. Doing the same thing over and over is easy.

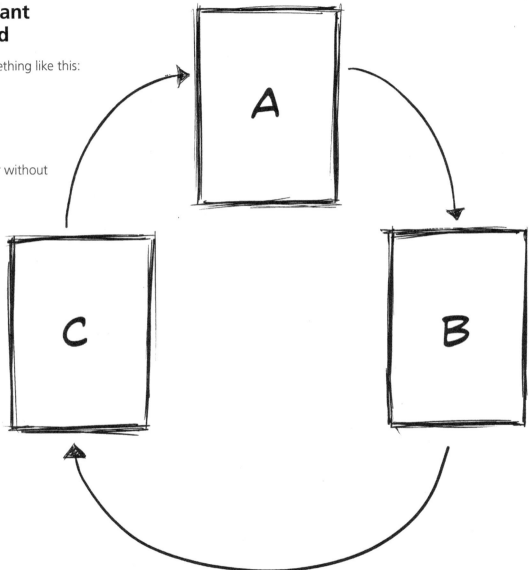

VII

Designing Behavior

Designing with Intention

As UX designers, we should always have goals in mind: our own and the users'. Unlike UI design, your UX skills (or lack thereof) are measured by how well you achieve those goals.

- You want users to do something.
- Users want to do something.
- Those two somethings might not be the same.

AS A UX DESIGNER

It is your job to make them the same. When the user completes their goal, you should also complete yours. That means you're not just designing random artwork; you have intentions. Stores intend to sell stuff. Social networks intend to create registrations and social interactions. Porn sites intend you to... well, you get the idea.

A visual designer—like a UI designer—designs the interface itself. That's important, but everyone has an opinion about how it looks. A lot of those opinions might be cryptic and useless, but still.

A UX designer designs how something works, i.e., the behavior of the users. You can't see behavior. But you can measure it.

UX Design Is Not a Matter of Opinion

One of the biggest new ideas when you get started with UX is the idea that you are now an active part of the design. You can predict and control what users choose, click, like, and do.

UX is the science of design. It's all about results. But to get good results, you need to motivate users to be more effective. This also means that one UX design can be "more right" than another, regardless of which one everybody likes better. And we can prove it. Sometimes even the users prefer the wrong one! (This is covered in Lesson 24.)

That can be a hard thing to accept, for many people.

Over the next five lessons, you will learn how to make people fight over imaginary things, drool when you ring a bell, how to "go viral," create addictive games, and create trust in your designs and content.

Rewards and Punishments

If psychology were math, this lesson would be when we move from adding and subtracting to multiplying and dividing. It's easy, but it allows you to design behavior that grows over time.

Feelings, Not Things

Most people are familiar with the general idea of a reward or a punishment. Reward = good. Punishment = bad. The part that a lot of people don't understand is that rewards and punishments are feelings, not things.

Your parents might have given you a toy for doing well in school, but the toy caused a happy feeling. Similarly, your parents might have taken away your bicycle because you started a meth business with your chemistry teacher, but it was the negative feeling that was the punishment, not the bicycle, and that feeling is what we're interested in.

i.e., Rewards and punishments are emotions. You can cause those emotions in a million different ways.

Feedback to Yourself

The mind-blowing part about emotions is that they are your brain giving feedback to your brain about something that happened. INCEPTION.

But since you, the designer, can control what happens, that means you can control the feedback. Which means you can train your users by rewarding them for something you consider good, and punish them for something you consider bad. That is a powerful thing. It's how we learned everything we know.

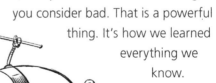

Learning = Associations = Beliefs

The last really fundamental piece in our psychological model is the concept of associations. Over time, we can learn to feel positively or negatively about anything: your favorite colors, your lucky number, and the type of people you find attractive are all examples.

You "associate" those things with positive feelings, because they have been relevant when you experienced rewards in the past. Even if those associations are actually just superstitions (false beliefs). Punishments work the same way with negative associations. That's how beliefs—including religions—are made, baby! So if your goal in this course is to start a cult, you'll love the next few lessons.

If you have ever wondered why people spend hours per day on Facebook but nobody could be bothered to use Google+, now you know.

Conditioning and Addiction

Your job as a UX designer is to create experiences, not just observe them. So we need to do more than reward and punish what users naturally do. We need the science of training people to do something new, and then keep doing it. Forever.

"The First Taste Is Free"

As any good drug dealer knows, nobody can be addicted to something they haven't tried. So your mission is to get the user to a positive emotion within a minute or less, on the first visit. This is so important, in my opinion, that you should not launch anything until you achieve it.

IMPORTANT

A "punishment" doesn't have to be painful. Think of it as a cost. It could be effort or money. People will do a little work or pay a little cash to get a reward, if the reward is worth it. *But*, the first reward should be free. Always.

Types of conditioning

Classical

Connect a signal of your choice to an existing behavior. For example, when a bell rings, food comes out. Food makes dogs drool. After the bell becomes strongly associated with food, the bell will make a dog expect food and drool all over himself. Therefore, the bell now causes drooling. And if drooling is your goal (that would be a weird app), you can trigger it any time you want.

Operant

Reward or punish a random action. Let's say you find a new website and write a comment. Ten people like it. Cool. You write another comment. Five more likes. Wow! Now you're hooked. You write a third. Somebody calls you an idiot. Hmmm. No more comments like that, I guess. The next one will be more like the first two. Six likes! Now you're being trained.

Type of rewards and punishments

You can reward someone by giving something good or taking away something bad.

If you do something good, I can give you a treat. Or I can stop putting dog poo in your shoes. Either way, your experience gets better.

Both work.

However, if you do 100 things I like, you will have 100 treats. Or, you could just have your shoes, still without poo in them.

AS A UX DESIGNER

Focus on giving so there is a sense of progress over time. Plus, your users will become loyal instead of resenting you.

Shape Their Behavior

Big, complex behavior starts small. Want your pigeon to learn bowling? No problem. Reward it when it goes near the ball. Punish it when it moves away. Then, demand more. It must touch the ball to get the reward now. Then it has to push the ball to get a reward. And so on.

Eventually the pigeon will be giving high-fives and drinking beer with the team. (This was actually done as a real experiment, by real psychologists, and no pigeons were harmed. I admit, I was a bit jealous of their bowling scores.)

Timing Matters

How often does your design reward the user?

Regularly

If users are rewarded every time or "every X times," they will begin to feel like they deserve it. Like a salary. It is hard to take that away, but it is also hard for users to walk away. Over time it gets boring, though, and it creates quantity, not quality. If your design can't function without something, like the economy needs money in real life, then guaranteed rewards-for-work is useful.

Randomly

Slot machines will reward you often enough that you get hooked, but the rewards are unpredictable. This can be the most addictive, because there is always a chance that "the next one might be the big one."

AS A UX DESIGNER

Random rewards based on the quality of content—like blogging or social media comments—will raise the level of content overall. If users cannot control rewards—like slot machines—it's just as effective but makes them more selfish.

Make It Addictive

Up until now we have talked about rewards and punishments as if you only do one or the other. But what if doing an action gets a reward, and not doing that action gets a punishment?

People presumably try drugs because they make you feel good the first time. However, after a while, not doing the drug makes you feel terrible. You can't stop.

That's addiction. Or *FarmVille*. In *FarmVille*, it was easy to get started, and if you keep playing, your farm becomes big and successful. However, if you stop playing, your crops die and your work is ruined— unless you invite your friends… or pay.

Gamification

The difference between a game and a nongame has nothing to do with badges and points. It's all about the psychology. Game design can be very nuanced, but let's start with some fundamentals.

One of the trendiest things in UX over the past few years have been the idea of adding "game mechanics" to things that aren't actually games. One thing that games do very well is structuring rewards and punishments in a way that leads users through a series of goals. If you want to do that, too, you came to the right place.

You will learn two major elements of game design:

- Feedback Loops
- Progressive Challenges

What Is a Feedback Loop?

A feedback loop has three ingredients: motivation, an action, and the feedback (emotion).

The user's motivation might exist already, or it could be something you design for them, like beating Bowser in *Mario Kart*. That smug bastard.

Once the user is motivated, they need a way to act. This is when you start the race, or show them the problem to solve, or give them a place to type their comment, or whatever. Then, they need feedback: an evaluation, or score, or Likes, or real-time race positions, or something else that informs the user how effective they were/are.

Loop it

It's called a feedback "loop" because the feedback should be something that motivates the user to do the action again. Maybe they will try to beat their old score, or maybe they didn't quite win this time, or maybe other people loved what they did.

Progressive Challenges

It's nice if a game is really easy at first so new users can jump right in. But once people know how the game works, it's not about just getting it done anymore. It's about getting it done better. To create progression, you merely have to create a bigger, better, harder way to do what the user already knows.

The idea of "progression" is the reason for levels in *Super Mario*, or badges in *Foursquare*, or campaigns in *Battlefield*, or stars in *Angry Birds*. Any goal that is more difficult than the previous goal.

Often, companies will make you pay to access the higher levels, because now you're addicted. A Game/UX designer did that. And you should, too.

Game Mechanics Are Motivations and Emotions

Feedback loops take your brain's natural or "implicit" motivation and make it an external or "explicit" motivation by using symbols in the game. Rewards and punishments are feelings, not things. It's how you trigger them that matters.

Badges and points are one way. Followers and Retweets are another. Friends and Likes, your job title and salary, and your street address and type of car—all symbols of progression.

Progression uses your motivation for status to make you "level up," over and over. It's the motivation to win, to improve, or to be better than Bowser. That arrogant son-of-a-bitch.

Social/Viral Structure

The Internet is famous for making things "go viral" but if your site isn't designed to create viral word-of-mouth, it won't. In this lesson, we'll learn how to translate emotional content into viral popularity.

Virality Is Much More Than Sharing: It's a Feature

If you are working on a social network or an app with social features, or your site is based on user-submitted content, or if your dream is to be the next Grumpy Cat, this is for you.

The Basic Formula

Action from User A = Feedback for User B = Content for User C

For example:

- You share a friend's photo on Facebook. That's your action, which gives feedback to your friend. When you share it, the rest of your friends see the photo in their feed, with a note saying you shared it.

- You retweet something on Twitter. The original tweeter gets the feedback. Your followers see the tweet in their feed, from you.

- You pin something on Pinterest. The original pinner gets feedback. Your followers see the pin in their feed, from you.

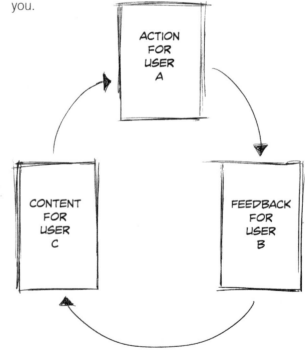

And so on.

Then, even more people see it, do actions, which give feedback, and creates even more content…

Ta da! More viral than a group of toddlers with the flu.

However, Facebook doesn't show Likes to very many people, like it does with a Share. And Twitter doesn't show Favorites to people like a Retweet. And Pinterest doesn't show Likes to people like a Pin.

It's ok to have actions that don't create Viral Loops, but they should usually be lower priority visually in your design—the second choice; or third.

Facebook's Share links are way too small and quiet (visually), and Share is the last one in the list. Twitter's Reply and Retweet are first in the list, but still visually quiet. Pinterest's Pin button is obvious and red and on the left.

Facebook sucks for virality. Twitter is better (within a short time frame). Pinterest is even better (for images). Surprised?

Why Does This Work?

Viral structure achieves a few things when done right:

2-in-1 actions

The user who originally does the action does it for themselves. Always. Virality is an automatic machine that translates your emotional actions into more content.

Good shit floats

This type of feature turns your design into a "quality content" machine. The more actions people do on a piece of content, the more visible it gets. But content that nobody likes, disappears.

Social proof

It shows people that someone relevant liked it. Hopefully many relevant people. Then, affiliation kicks in.

Self-promotion

Since everyone can see who shared something, it creates an incentive to share more, to make yourself more visible (Status).

Network saturation

When everyone you know believes something, you are much more likely to believe it, too.

How to Create Trust

In UX design, it can be easy to slip into all the structures and techniques and forget about the fact that users are real people and they can tell when you're full of shit. Context matters. Honesty matters.

Trust Is a Critical Element in Everything You Do

There are lots of ways to create trust, but when users don't trust your design, your perspective often prevents you from realizing it.

Here are seven simple ideas that are always worth considering:

1. Professionalism

    This might seem obvious, but you need to look like a real company (i.e., not a scam). Part of that is visual design, part isn't. Real companies will protect your data, survive until next year, and send you the stuff you just paid for. Companies often focus all their attention on the sales team and advertising; meanwhile, their website is five years old and wasn't very good in the first place. That hurts trust.

2. Nothing is 100% positive or negative

    Top-rated product reviews are both positive and negative. It has also been shown that app ratings and book reviews are most-trusted when they do not have all 5-star ratings. A few 3- or 4-star ratings actually increase sales. Real people feel suspicious when something seems "too perfect."

3. Democratize

    As a group your users can be like a quality filter. Some companies use artificial intelligence to identify good content or prevent fraud, when they could be using actual intelligence. If you build voting and rating tools that are hard to abuse (limit the number of votes, require some experience to vote, etc.), what you have actually done is identify what your users trust most.

4. Accountability

Trust can be built by showing information *and* by hiding it. Real names and contact information can reduce the amount of hateful, aggressive comments you get, and can make a company feel more personal. However, hiding someone's identity will make them more comfortable with sharing private or embarrassing information. And doing the opposite will get the opposite result. Showing that you understand the consequences of information will create trust.

5. Handle negativity with grace

Many people panic when they get negative feedback in public, but you shouldn't. When a company receives negative feedback and then deals with it gracefully in public they actually build more trust than positive feedback does. So pause, be thoughtful, and focus on solving the user's problem instead of protecting your ego.

6. Keep users informed

So simple, yet so neglected. Think about what users need to make a purchase or register. Will there be shipping costs? Will you share my email address? Will I get spam? Will you charge my credit card immediately? Just tell them up front! It is better to tell the truth than let the user worry about it. Even when the truth isn't the answer the users wants.

7. Use simple words

It is a myth that complicated language makes you more persuasive. Just speak like a normal person would speak. The more complicated you get, the fewer people will understand. Nobody trusts what they don't understand.

How Experience Changes Experience

New users and experienced users will see your design differently.

Power Users Are the Minority

Statistically-speaking, it is impossible for advanced or power users to be "most" of the people using your design; although it can be very tempting to believe that.

Unless your product/service is highly technical, the vast majority of your users will be normal people with other stuff to do. Not super-focused, tech-savvy people like you and your colleagues.

HARD TRUTH

If you want millions of happy users, design for the distracted idiots, not the obsessed geniuses.

Hidden versus Visible: The Paradox of Choice

In most projects, there will be situations where you have to decide how "clean" you want your layout to be. Designers will usually choose to hide everything because it looks better. Non-designers will want all of their favorite features to be visible all of the time, which will be a different set of features for each person.

So, how do you choose?

Visible features will always be used more and discovered more than hidden features. We are reminded that they exist every time we see them. However, the "Paradox of Choice" says the more options you see, the less likely you are to choose any of them. So, if you overload normal users with too many choices, they will freak out and run away screaming.

Make sure beginners can find the core features easily. Ideally, without clicking anything. And try to give power users easy access to advanced features, even if they aren't visible all the time.

Recognition versus Memory

How many different icons could you name off the top of your head, right now? How many could you recognize if I gave you a list? If you're a normal human, the second answer would be a lot more.

If you design your interface so people have to ask for something—like search—they will only use the features they can remember. This means that, over time, they will use fewer and fewer features. Not more and more.

If your users are forced to deal with a large amount of information, give them some suggestions of categories or some other kind of help to remind them where to look!

Learning Is Slow; Habits Are Fast

"Onboarding" is the word we use to describe the step-by-step lessons or very simple introductions to a new interface. It helps new users find the main features easily, and avoid confusion. However, what happens when the user has used your interface for two years?

Habits are created very quickly in your users' minds, so you should design a "fast way" to do key features, which might not be as obvious. Power users will take the time to learn them for the sake of extra productivity. Keyboard shortcuts, right-click options, and all the little Twitter tricks like ".@" tweets are examples of this idea.

VIII

Visual Design Principles

Visual Weight (Contrast and Size)

This lesson is the first of five visual principles that will help you direct the user's attention. Some parts of your design are more important than others, so we have to help users notice the important stuff.

The idea of visual weight is fairly intuitive. Some things look "heavier" than others in a layout. They draw your attention more easily. And that idea is valuable to a UX designer. Your job is to help users notice the things that matter. And it is equally important not to distract the users from their goals.

By adding visual "weight" to certain parts of your design, you increase the chance that a user will see them and you change where their eyes will go next. Remember: visual weight is relative. All visual principles are about comparing a design element to whatever is around it.

So, without further ado, I would like to introduce you to the stars of the UX Crash Course: The Rubber Ducks! *applause here*

Contrast

The difference between light things and dark things is called *contrast*. The more distinguishable a light thing is compared to a dark thing, the "higher" the contrast.

In UX, you want to give important things higher contrast, like the duck in the center. In this case, most of the image is light, so a dark duck is more noticeable. If the image were mostly dark, the lighter duck would be more noticeable.

If these were buttons, more people would click the dark one than if all the buttons were the same color.

THE CENTER DUCK DRAWS YOUR EYE MOST. CONTRAST EFFECTS VISUAL WEIGHT.

Depth and Size

In the real world, we notice things that are close to us more than things that are far away.

In the digital world, bigger things are perceived to be closer, like the middle duck in the second illustration, and something that is smaller is perceived to be farther away (like the blurry duck in the back.) If the ducks were all the same size, you would probably look at them from left to right (assuming you read that way). If you use blur effects or shadows it just makes the perception of depth more realistic. Size has this effect even if your design looks "flat."

As a general rule, you want more important things to be bigger than less important things. This creates a visual "hierarchy" on the page and makes it easier to scan, but it also allows you to choose what the user notices first. That's why it's wrong to "make the logo bigger," unless you want users to stare at your logo instead of buying something.

THE FRONT, CENTER DUCK ATTRACTS MORE ATTENTION. DEPTH AND SIZE CHANGE VISUAL WEIGHT.

Color

Real life is full of sunlight, artificial light, heat, cold, clothing, brands, fashion, and a million other things that affect the way we perceive colors. As a UX designer, we might not care about Pantones and brand guidelines, but we definitely have to learn about color.

WHICH DUCK LOOKS COLD? OR LIKE A WARNING? COLOUR HAS MEANING.

WHICH DUCK SEEMS TO COME FORWARD? COLOUR CAN RECEDE OR ADVANCE.

There are a few things we can learn about color from the Technicolor rubber duckies on the preceding page. As UX designers, we usually rock the wireframes in black and white. And that's a good thing! We focus on the function, while the UI designers can focus on the look, feel, and style. However, sometimes color is function. Like traffic lights, or making the color of a popsicle match the flavor. You know, important shit.

Meaning

In the first illustration in this lesson, we see three ducks in different colors: blue, yellow, and red. They're so handsome. Immediately, these ducks seem to have different tonality, and it is easy to imagine how the colors can change what each duck "means."

If the ducks were buttons, they might be "confirm," "cancel," and "delete." If they were indicators on a fuel tank, they might represent "full," "half," and "empty." Or if they were on a stove: "cold," "warm," and "hot."

You get the idea: the ducks are identical, but colors change the meaning. If you don't need to indicate something like that, let the UI designer choose colors. But if you do, let your wireframes do the talking.

> **PROTIP**
> Don't argue with other designers about the specific *shade* of color. In UX, pale red and primary red are both red. That's all you care about.

Recede or Advance

The other thing to keep in mind is that colors can be "loud" or "quiet." The second image in Lesson 52 shows a red duck and two blueish ones. The red duck almost looks a little closer, doesn't it? It's not. Something like a "buy" button should have a color that makes it jump off the screen. More people will click a color that "advances" (comes forward).

On the other hand, sometimes we want things to step back so they are visible, but not too distracting, like the two blueish ducks. They "recede" (sink backward). This is good for something like a menu that is always on the screen. If it is always yelling at you, that's unnecessary and it steals focus from more important things.

Keep Wireframes Simple

Colorful wireframes just get in the way of the functional details. Use colors where they matter, but don't make your wireframes blue like blueprints, or dress them up for clients. It makes all discussions about color confusing: "No, the website won't be blue…"

Combine Visual Principles

Color can work really well with the previous lesson about Visual Weight. Something big is noticeable, but you can't miss something big and red! Make your errors and warning labels red and high contrast. Or, if you're just confirming what the user did, something a little smaller in a receding green might be perfect.

Repetition and Pattern-Breaking

One important visual design principle involves the creation of patterns to move the user's eyes to important things. And like all good rules, patterns are made to be broken.

THESE DUCKS CREATE A PATTERN. REPETITION CHANGES PERCEPTION.

Who knew we could learn so much from rubber ducks?!

Human brains have a particular talent for patterns and sequences. Whenever something in nature happens over and over, we will quickly notice. In fact, we don't just notice, we think about those things differently.

The first image shows five identical rubber ducks in a row. We don't see five individual ducks though, we see a row of ducks. We treat them as a group or a sequence, and if you live in the

Western world, you will probably look at them from left to right because that's how we read. If that row of ducks were a menu or a list, we would do the same thing. Therefore, you could expect more people to click the options on the left, and fewer people to click the options on the right.

Breaking a Pattern

The second image shows the same five rubber ducks (still lookin' good, aren't they?) but this time one of them has gone solo. We'll call her Beyoncé.

That changes everything. Now we see a row of four (jealous) ducks, and Beyoncé is alone, in the spotlight. She woke up like that! It is hard not to focus on Beyoncé, even though all five ducks are equally majestic creatures.

Now, if that were a menu, the middle option would get far more clicks than before because our eyes fixate on it. Also, those clicks would be stolen from the left options, so the left options would be less popular than before (although probably still more popular than the far-right option).

That's a powerful thing to know.

This might seem simple and obvious, but when you apply that principle to your designs—or your dance routines—it can make people notice the important buttons, options, or pop stars.

Be careful: pattern-breaking can also lead the user's eyes away from other important things. Before you can break a pattern, you have to make one.

Combine Your Principles

To make a pattern or a sequence, keep visual weight and color consistent. The user's eye will start at one end and follow the pattern to the other end. To break the pattern, just switch it up in the place where you want to add focus. Make the "Register Now" button an unexpected color, size, shape, or style, and watch your clicks go up overnight!

WHEREVER A PATTERN IS BROKEN, THAT'S WHERE WE FOCUS.

Line Tension and Edge Tension

Repetition, as we learned in the last lesson, creates a pattern. However, certain types of repetition can also create the perception of shapes that affect where the user's eyes will go.

YOU SEE A LINE OF DUCKS WITH A GAP. WHY DON'T YOU JUST SEE 8 DUCKS?

Are you tired of the ducks yet? I didn't think so.

Visual "tension" is a concept that seems very elementary, but you'd be amazed how useful it can be. Our brains are a little too good at seeing patterns where they don't exist. As a designer you can use that.

Line Tension

The first image shows eight ducks in a row. We don't see eight individual ducks; we see a line. That's line tension. The perception of a line or a "path" when there isn't one. Our eyes will follow the path to see where it goes. Super useful.

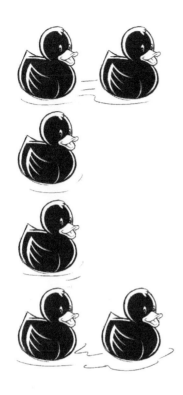

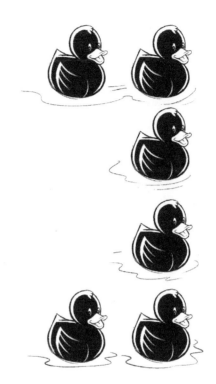

DO YOU SEE 12 DUCKS, OR A BOX MADE OF DUCKS? THAT'S EDGE TENSION.

If we break that path—like any broken pattern—the gap steals more focus.

Edge Tension

So far, we have assumed there is only one line. But what if we create line tension using more than one line?

The result can be "shapes."

In the second image, I have arranged the ducks so they appear to form the corners of a box. You could see 12 ducks, or four groups of 3 ducks, but your mind really wants to see the box, so it does. Furthermore, now we can put things "inside" the box (like more ducks!), or in the spaces between the corners. Similar to line tension, edge tension brings focus to the gaps.

Layout-wise, this can be an excellent way to put more focus on something small, like a label. Or you can create visual paths leading to the button you want people to click. Vintage ads use this technique often to put a small logo in focus. And conveniently, it makes a layout feel simpler and more cohesive because a path or a box is only one mental thing, but 12 separate ducks is too much awesome to handle.

Combine Your Principles

In this lesson I have left the "tension" gaps blank, but you don't have to. You can also use color to create a path like a gradient on a list of items. Or you can add visual weight to a group of elements by treating them like one shape instead of separate pieces. It's a great way to direct the user's eyes without adding any more things to a layout!

Alignment and Proximity

The last design principle you will learn about is how to add order and meaning to elements of your design without adding any more elements. It might sound subtle, but it affects everything you see, every day.

Alignment

In the first image you see a group of six stunningly beautiful ducks, but you also see a lot of relationships. because of the way they are aligned:

- We see two rows.

- The far-left and far-right ducks seem to be separated.

- The two center ducks seem the most organized.

- All ducks seem to be going in the same direction.

- If you see motion, the far-left duck might be falling behind.

- If you see motion, the far-right duck might be leading.

Those six ducks are identical. Only the alignment creates these perceptions. Buttons with similar functions can be aligned.

DUCKS THAT ARE ALIGNED SEEM MORE RELATED.

Different levels of content can be aligned. Information can be in a grid of rows and columns like a spreadsheet to create complex meaning.

Proximity

The closeness or distance between two objects creates a feeling of those objects being related or unrelated. That distance is called *proximity*.

In the second image, you see six identical ducks that are not aligned horizontally or vertically, but you definitely see two groups. The ducks in each group seem together, like a team or a family. The only thing creating that perception is their proximity.

In your designs, put related elements closer together and unrelated elements farther apart. For example: a headline, a block of text, and a button that are all related to one action—like a purchase or an app download—are usually designed like a "package." That allows the user to understand that they go together without reading anything.

THE CLOSER THE DUCKS ARE TO EACH OTHER, THE MORE RELATED THEY SEEM.

Using Motion for UX

In digital design, it is becoming more and more common to include animation or motion design as part of the UX. It's a stylish detail, but in UX, you care about more than style. Motion is a tool.

If Motion Makes People Wait, It's Bad

Before you start designing amazing transitions between screens, and smooth animated buttons, and parallax gravity in your scrolling, think about the user. If the user is trying to navigate, or if they know what is coming, or if they have to see this animation a hundred times every time they use your site or app, you might be doing more harm than good.

Animations take time to show, and making users wait quickly gets frustrating. Even worse than waiting, sometimes animations make things hard to read, or they distract users from the content and buttons you want them to read and click.

Motion Is Noticed First

If you have ever been disturbed by a vibrating banner or a jumping button, then you understand how motion can draw your attention. If you made a list of the things your brain notices, in order of priority, motion would be first. But, a little goes a long way. If you make a vibrating banner or a jumping button (which are really annoying to click, by the way) I will hunt you down and... well... let's just say it won't be pretty.

Straight lines point in a direction

Different types of motion will do different things to the user's eyes. If you make something move in a straight line, the user's brain will anticipate where it's going and the user will look at the "end of the line." If you are using motion to highlight key features or tell users where to go, straight lines are a good choice.

STRAIGHT-LINE

Curved lines make people follow the curve

However, if you want to lead users around the screen—like when you're explaining your app for the first time—curved motion will make their eyes stick to the path and stop where the animation stops.

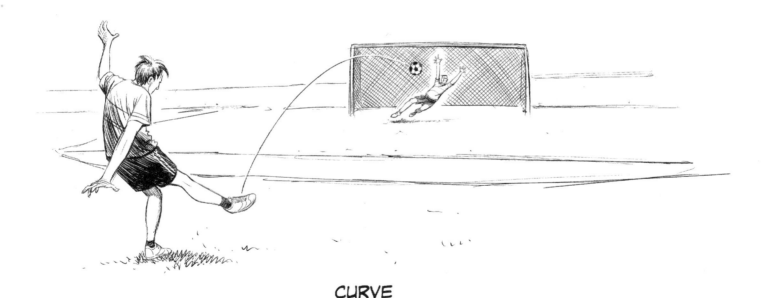

CURVE

IX

Wireframes and Prototypes

What Is a Wireframe?

Wireframes are important, if not essential. If we are the "architect," wireframes are the blueprints. But their simple appearance makes some people think they are simple, easy documents.

A wireframe is a technical document. Lines, boxes, labels. Maybe a color or two. That's it.

Wireframes are often compared to blueprints because they have a similar purpose. A blueprint tells builders how to execute the architect's plan. Not which wallpaper or furniture to choose. And blueprints are taken seriously. They aren't a suggestion, or a "rough sketch," or a "quick mock up." All those sketches you make on whiteboards or during brainstorming sessions are valuable, but they aren't wireframes. They are your thoughts about the wireframes you will make later.

A wireframe might only take an hour to draw, but it can take weeks or months to plan. It is important that your colleagues and clients understand that. If another developer or

designer can't use your wireframe yet, it isn't a wireframe. It's a sketch. Keep going.

What Isn't a Wireframe?

When most people think of UX, they think of the lines-and-boxes diagrams we call wireframes. Unfortunately, many people also think that doing wireframes is the same as doing UX.

A wireframe *is* a planning document. It *is* a technical instruction document for the "builders." Wireframes allow us to say insightful stuff like, "Oops, I forgot the main menu!" in the same way an architect could say, "Oops, I forgot the front door!"

Still, many people have a broad misunderstanding of wireframes and use them incorrectly. The following is a list of what wireframes are not. See if you recognize yourself in any of the Top 5 *unforgivable* (!) wireframe sins:

1. Wireframes are not a basic sketch.

   Often we treat wireframes like a quick and dirty sketch, or like step 1 of the design. "Just make a wireframe for now!" They aren't. Wireframes specifically exclude design, to show how the site/app will work, not how it will look. Those napkin drawings you (and I) make at the beginning are important for sorting out our thoughts, but they're not wireframes.

   Explain early concepts/thoughts in words and pictures, not with wireframes. Show flows as icons, hand-drawn sketches, site maps, slides, or user stories instead; they're better, faster to make, and easier for the client to understand.

2. Good wireframes take time.

   I know they look basic, but there is a lot of thinking behind those empty rectangles. Every little piece must be planned and placed carefully on a specific page. Every link needs a destination. Every page needs a link (on another page) to get there. Every button needs to be where the user needs it, not where the user doesn't need it. Wireframes are 90% thinking, 10% drawing. Make sure everyone respects the need for the 90% part!

3. Wireframes aren't presented in phases.

   Everything made by humans goes through "drafts" as we perfect our ideas, but wireframes are either ready or they're not. If they're not finished it is because something isn't solved, isn't organized, won't work, will be hard to use, or is missing. If you can't start to build, the wireframes are a work in progress. Don't be afraid to say that to a client or your manager! Making decisions based on half-ready wireframes is a nightmare waiting to happen. I say this from experience.

4. Wireframes should be taken seriously.

I have watched people move a printed wireframe (on paper) from one section of a site to another because it "feels" better. I have seen a 70-page set of wireframes for a social network that didn't have a profile page (designed by one of the top ad agencies in the world!). I have seen user-generated content that cannot be generated anywhere. I have seen a client cross out a "register now" button because it's "ugly" in the wireframe. I have seen a site designed and launched by a global agency without a main menu (you thought I was joking when I said that, didn't you?).

These might or might not seem like a big deal, but each is an example of a crippling mistake that could destroy a product or service.

Plan enough time for wireframes—especially in large projects. Label and describe (i.e., annotate) each element of each page so a developer never has to ask you what a button is supposed to do.

5. Wireframes are not meant for display.

I die a little every time I see wireframes colored blue and presented in a stylish way. Immediately I know that the people behind those wireframes have no respect for what they're doing: they have not used color with meaning (red for warning, etc.), they have tried to pass important things by a client/ boss by making them prettier, and they have put the focus on the "look-and-feel" in a document that is primarily for technical purposes. Making a wireframe look like a blueprint is the equivalent of using Comic Sans to write a contract.

Learn Skills, Not Tools

One of the most common questions in UX is "What is the best wireframing tool?" But when you get good at wireframing, you will realize that the answer to that question is: the simplest one.

A lot of designers are surprised when I tell them that I use Adobe Illustrator, Sketch, and Apple Keynote to do wireframes (unless the project is really complex).

I have used Omnigraffle, Mockflow, Balsamiq, and a variety of other software options, which might or might not have been intended for wireframes, and to be honest, I think most of them are too complicated, most of the time.

Different Tools Work in Different Situations

If you're making a very complex site with a lot of different content, like a giant, international corporate intranet for a company with tens of thousands of employees, then you might need a powerful tool.

But for most projects, those tools might be overkill.

I have designed entire social networks that are responsive, in a web-based drawing tool. I have designed iPad apps with six-figure budgets in Keynote. I have designed a website for a leading cable television channel, completely in Illustrator.

All without complaints.

My advice: find and use the simplest tool that can handle the project and make files that your team can share easily and cheaply.

They're wireframes, not the Mona Lisa.

Design the Best Solution, Not the Solution the Tool Can Design

No matter what type of design you do, you should always make sure you are doing the design based on the solution you need, not based on the features you have in your software.

Always design what you want first, and then use wireframes to make it into a technical document. If you start solving problems with a blank wireframing tool, you're screwed before you start.

Often a pencil and paper is the best wireframing tool.

My first recommendation to all new UX designers is to use a pencil and paper for wireframing until you need to be so specific and technically accurate that something digital is required.

Sketch quickly, make rough drawings of your ideas, try 10 different versions, sort out your layouts and ideas, decide on something, and *then* jump onto your computer to make a formal document.

Avoid Convenient Examples

One of the most common design mistakes is to forget about less common user behavior. If you only use ideal content in your wireframes, your design might break in real life.

If your design works well for 90% of users, it's broken.

In my experience, conversations about UX design focus on the way you *want* users to use your stuff, not the way they *could* use it. That's dangerous.

If you hear yourself saying things like, "Most headlines will probably fit on one line," or "Users probably won't have more than a thousand friends anyway," or "Most of our users will probably use their face as a profile picture," you're creating opportunities for failure.

How Short Can It Be?

What if someone chooses a period as a title? Or leaves it blank? Or makes a one-word description? Or, what if their whole blog is just single word posts?

It is tempting to imagine everybody doing normal things, but people are creative and weird. Maybe they are writing articles about punctuation or maybe they run a "word of the day" blog, or maybe they don't need one of your features. On Pinterest, people regularly "skip" the description by typing a single period. If you need users to click that text to navigate, they are now trying to click a single period.

How Long Can It Be?

This is the more common mistake when designing: to forget the really long possibilities.

In 1999, singer/songwriter Fiona Apple's second album title was an entire poem. I have seen a trademarked company name that is 40 words long. I have seen a blog where the whole post is in the title and the "body text" is always blank.

If you're designing a music site, or a trademark list, or a blog template, would those behaviors still work, or would your design break?

What If It Doesn't Exist?

It is surprisingly common to forget the "empty state" of a design. What does the page look like if a user hasn't posted anything yet? Don't just let it be empty; design what it looks like if it is empty.

What If Someone Deletes It?

The more difficult version of "empty" is "deleted." On Reddit, a user can post a comment, and other users can reply to it, and then the original user can delete the first comment in the conversation.

What would happen in your design if something like that happened? What if someone has shared a link to something that is deleted? What does the user see when they visit that link?

What's the Worst That Can Happen?

Don't ask yourself what most users will do. That's the easy part. Ask yourself how a user could *abuse* your design the most. Limit the number of characters they can type, or design it so it looks ok with *only* a title, or *no title*, or take away

the button that lets them delete the post, or add an ellipsis (the three periods at the end) when it gets too long (that's called *truncating*!), or add a little note if the user edits the original content so other people know it changed.

And test your design with a lot of ugly, unusual images! You'll thank me when the Naked Ninja Association creates their account.

What Is a Design Pattern?

When many designers have the same challenge and someone solves it in an elegant way, and many designers use that solution, it is called a *design pattern*.

A design is not necessarily good just because it's common. To be a "good" design pattern, a solution must be common and usable.

Some design ideas become popular because they allow lazy UI designers to ignore a challenging feature. It's like putting a bag over someone's head because they are ugly.

For example: Facebook's "hamburger" button—which represents the hidden menu in many mobile apps—has started appearing on full-size websites that have plenty of space for a menu. It's common because hiding the menu is easier than designing a nice one, not because the results are better.

In real life, many users don't notice the hidden "hamburger" menu button at all, and they leave the site or get lost.

That's bad.

And lazy.

"Don't do it, bitch."—Jesse Pinkman.

Now, there are hundreds of design patterns, and they are changing all the time as devices and technologies evolve, so I can't really make you a full list. But if you google "UI design patterns," you will find many sites that collect common solutions (whether they are good or not).

Z-Pattern, F-Pattern, Visual Hierarchy

It is easy to imagine every user excitedly reading every letter you write and every pixel you make. Get over it, because real users won't. They *scan*.

"Scanning" means the user only stops to read when something catches their eye. This lesson is about scanning patterns.

Using a website or an app may feel like a different experience every time, but in fact, the way people look at any design is fairly predictable.

The Z-Pattern

Let's start with the most boring design I can imagine: an entire newspaper page of solid text. All one story. No headlines. No images. No breaks or pull quotes; just text, in even columns, from corner to corner.

In a design like that—which I hope you never create—users will generally scan it in a pattern something like a "Z," starting in the upper left and ending in the lower right. Anything in the layout that isn't near the Z probably won't be noticed.

Boring! Zzzzzzzz…. (see what I did there?)

The reason I spent so much time teaching you visual design principles is so you would know how you can make this layout better.

Aha!

If we add a bigger headline (visual weight), create one column to follow (line tension), and use smaller sections (repetition), we can get people closer to the famous F-Pattern.

F-Pattern

Similar layouts = similar scanning pattern. Google results make a great F-Pattern if you track the eye movements of users.

The F-Pattern made the founders of the Nielsen Norman Group famous a while back. They still maintain a very good blog and publish many reports worth reading.

The F-Pattern works like this:

1. Start in the upper-left corner, like the Z-Pattern.

2. Read/scan the first (head)line of the text.

3. Scan down the left side of the column until you find something interesting.

4. Read the interesting thing more carefully.

5. Continue scanning down.

6. By repeating that method over and over, the scanning pattern starts to look like an "E" or an "F," hence the name.

Why Is This Important?

You might notice that some parts of the page get lots of attention "naturally," whereas other parts of the page are overlooked most of the time. This is what is meant by "strong" and "weak" spots in a layout.

A button in the *upper left* will get more clicks than a button in the *upper right*, which will get more clicks than a button in the *lower left*, which will get more clicks than a button in the *lower right*. And all of those will get more clicks than something randomly stuck in the middle, *unless you do something about it.*

It might also be good to know that each "block" of content and each column can have their own F-Pattern. It doesn't have to be one-F-Pattern-per-page, but that is a more advanced conversation for another day.

Create a Visual Hierarchy

When you consistently use typography to indicate the importance of text, and certain colors to highlight buttons, and when you give more visual weight to things that matter, it creates a visual hierarchy (i.e.,a design that people can scan easily). Our eyes jump from important thing to important thing rather than scanning like a robot.

Some designers think visual hierarchy is good because it looks better, but the truth is that it *feels* better because it is easier to scan.

Layout: Page Framework

Now that you've established your goals, researched your users, and planned your information architecture, it's time to put those plans into action!

Although it might be tempting to approach your wireframes on a page-by-page basis, don't do it!

If you're building a house, you don't start with the rooms and furniture. You start with the walls. This is one of those "measure twice, cut once" kind of things. As a general rule, you should do your wireframes like you do your tattoos: start with the big parts, then fill in the details. In this case the big parts are the elements that will appear on all of the pages: navigation and footers.

Footers

A footer is typically a list of static links that are too general and too insignificant to get a place in the main navigation. Some sites actually have really nice footer designs, which is great, but if users need those links to make the site work, the footer is the wrong place for them.

Ask yourself: "Are there going to be any pages that have an infinite scroll?" If the answer is yes, make sure everything in the footer is available somewhere else. If the language selector is in the footer and it runs away every time I try to change it, fuck you.

Navigation

Menus come in at least two flavors: main menu and submenu.

Main Menu

If you did your information architecture properly, then you already know what should be in the main menu. It's the first level of links in your site map (below the home page).

The order of the menu items—left-to-right or top-to-bottom—should be from most-to-least popular (measured by user interest, not by how much you like them).

If this is a brand new menu just make your best guess, and tell the developers that you want it to be easy to re-order them later. When you get some real traffic to your site, make sure your order and the real popularity match. If they don't, fix it.

Submenu

The submenu is a list of the pages in your site map "below" whatever page the user is on. You did make a site map, right?! Phew. Good. You had me scared for a second there.

The main thing with the submenu is that it should ideally be in the same place on every page, even if the links change all the time. That way, users will quickly learn where to find it.

Huge Submenus Are Never a Good Idea

I am always surprised when someone tries to argue that their mega-menu is the best idea available. That actually means the Information Architecture (and the information architect) sucks.

Everything-in-one-menu is the laziest design in the universe. Do better.

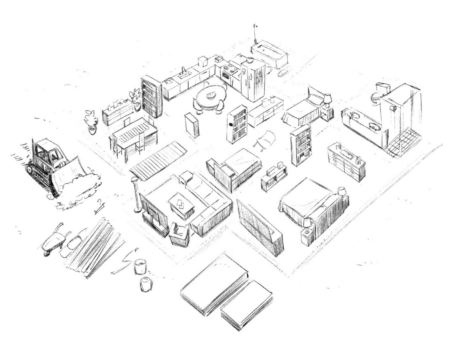

Menus are like dating: if you need more than seven or eight choices, it's time to break somebody's heart—maybe your own.

tl;dr

Create navigation and footers that work for all of the pages/screens in your app before you get into content. You'll thank me later.

Layout: The Fold, Images, and Headlines

There are many common questions about UX design that you will get throughout your career. And some that you should get, even though you won't.

The Fold

One of the most popular old-school misconceptions is about "the fold." In case you've never heard of it, this is the part of your design that is visible before the user scrolls. Everything above the fold will get maximum visibility. However, from the studies I have seen, 60 to 80% of users will scroll immediately if they expect to find something useful below the fold.

Whatever is above the fold should inform users about what is below the fold. If users don't know what is down there, they might not be interested enough to find out.

Careful: It is popular right now to use huge background images at the top of the page. If it looks like the site ends at the fold, people might leave instead of scrolling. And if you need to add a graphic that says "scroll down," your design is weak.

To learn more about the fold, go to *http://thereisnofold. tumblr.com/*.

Images

Many UX designers treat images as if they are not functional, but images can lead the user's eyes, so you should think about them.

Images of people, specifically, draw more attention than anything else you can use in your layout. As a general guideline, the more emotion an image adds, the more engaging it is.

- Choose images that add emotion and direct the user's eyes.

- Use headlines to direct users to what matters most.

Headlines

Other than pictures of people, our eyes are most attracted to the largest, highest-contrast piece of text in a layout. So when you add a big headline to your design, you have just chosen where people will begin scanning.

Therefore, it is important that your headline is aligned with the most important content below it. If that content is not very important, you will draw too much attention to it (and away from other content.) If it is not aligned, users will look for a new focus point after they read the headline.

tl;dr

- Give people something to focus on before they scroll.

- Make it obvious that they can scroll.

MADE YOU LOOK!

Layout: The Axis of Interaction

One of the most common questions in UX design is "Should the button be on the left or the right?" Well, it depends, actually. It depends on where you have created visual "edges."

This idea is deceptively simple.

Human attention is very limited. We can only focus on one thing at a time, like a squirrel, or Duck Dynasty, or a skimpy swimsuit. So while we're focusing on one chunk of content, the other chunks of content effectively become invisible.

Don't believe me? _See if you can pass this Selective Attention test._

FUN FACT

In photos of a man and woman in skimpy swimsuits, eye-tracking studies show that _women_ will look at the woman's breasts more than men, and _men_ will look at the man's crotch more than women. It's not about being sexy, it's about checking out the competition in nature.

Find the Edges

In every design, you will use the visual principles you learned in this course. When you step back and look at your layout, you will notice that you have created "lines" or "edges" or "blocks" everywhere.

They might be the aligned edge of the text, or your images, or groups of things in a row. Each of those edges is an _Axis of Interaction_. Your eyes will follow an Axis until it is interrupted or until it ends. Your user's attention is almost always focused on an Axis of Interaction, and when they stop focusing there, they will hop to the next Axis of Interaction.

Therefore, if you want people to click something, put it on (or near) an Axis of Interaction. If you don't want them to click it, put it somewhere else. The farther an element is from the Axis, the less people will see it, and if you don't see something, you can't click it.

THIS IS AN EXAMPLE.

LOREM IPSUM DOLOR SIT AMET, MELIUS
TRACTATOS INCORRUPTE NAM EI, ET HAS MUNERE
GRAECI ADIPISCI. AN VEL MOLESTIE TORQUATOS,
ET MODUS PERCIPIT EOS, AT ERREM ORATIO NEC.
ERROR ELOQUENTIAM EX SEA, PETENTIUM
MAIESTATIS ET SIT, PRI ID UTAMUR MOLESTIAE.
EUM AT DISCERE SIGNIFERUMQUE, VOCIBUS
PLATONEM NE EST. PRO EXERCI LEGIMUS ID, EI
SED IGNOTA IRIURE PROMPTA. QUI EI NOVUM
BLANDIT ATOMORUM, VEL APPETERE PATRIOQUE
MNESARCHUM CU, CU AUTEM APPELLANTUR VIX.

LOREM IPSUM DOLOR SIT AMET, MELIUS
TRACTATOS INCORRUPTE NAM EI, ET HAS MUNERE
GRAECI ADIPISCI. AN VEL MOLESTIE TORQUATOS,
ET MODUS PERCIPIT EOS, AT ERREM ORATIO NEC.
ERROR ELOQUENTIAM EX SEA, PETENTIUM
MAIESTATIS ET SIT, PRI ID UTAMUR MOLESTIAE.
EUM AT DISCERE SIGNIFERUMQUE, VOCIBUS
PLATONEM NE EST. PRO EXERCI LEGIMUS ID, EI
SED IGNOTA IRIURE PROMPTA. QUI EI NOVUM
BLANDIT ATOMORUM, VEL APPETERE PATRIOQUE
MNESARCHUM CU, CU AUTEM APPELLANTUR VIX.

| BUTTON HERE... | ...OR HERE... | ...OR HERE... | ...OR HERE? |

THE *AXIS OF INTERACTION* IS THE IMAGINARY "EDGE" YOUR EYE FOLLOWS NATURALLY.
THE CLOSER SOMETHING IS TO THE AXIS, THE MORE VISIBLE IT IS TO THE USER.

Forms

As you work through your designs, it is only a matter of time until you have to design a way for users to give you information. Forms are one of the places you will spend a lot of your time, usability-wise. They cause confusion, mistakes, and loss of engagement, and they are one of the most valuable parts of your site.

If they aren't one of the most valuable parts of your design, why are you using a form? Did I mention that they cause confusion, mistakes, and loss of engagement?

One Long Page or a Few Short Pages?

The most common question with regard to forms—from UX designers and marketers alike—is "How long is too long?"

It is a good general rule to keep forms as short as possible, but don't be afraid to break it into pages if it makes sense, or if you want to save the input in steps just in case the user quits in the middle. The main thing is to make a form *feel* simple. Keep related questions together; eliminate questions you don't really need; and use as many pages as you need, no more, no less.

Input Types

The purpose of a form is to get input (i.e., information from the user). And there are a number of ways you can collect it. Whether you use a standard text field or a super-custom slider, you should choose the input type that gives you the highest quality answers.

For example, let's say you want the user to pick their favorite type of goat. Checkboxes and radio buttons are both ways to let the user pick from a list of options. However, checkboxes allow them to choose more than one option, and radio buttons only allow one selection.

List of different form input types: *http://www.w3schools.com/htmL/html_form_input_types.asp*

List of different breeds of goats: *https://en.wikipedia.org/wiki/List_of_goat_breeds*

If you want a more complete answer from the user, use checkboxes. If you want a more selective answer, radio buttons might be your thing.

Labels and Instructions

When you're labeling your inputs—how else will the user know what to do with them?—be short, clear, legible, and put the labels close to the input. In the grand scheme of things, that will solve 99% of labeling problems.

Sometimes instructions are needed if the question is unconventional or complicated. In that case, it can be helpful to add a little explanation. If it's only a few words, put it near the label and the input. If it's more than a few words, put it on the side of the form instead of within it so it doesn't interrupt the flow of users who know what they're doing.

For more on this, I highly recommend the book *Web Form Design*, by Luke W.

Preventing and Handling Mistakes

When it comes to forms, mistakes happen. It's your job to prevent as many as possible and handle the rest as gracefully as you can.

You can prevent mistakes by adding some intelligence to the inputs. For example, if a text field is for phone numbers, make the form smart enough to handle the structure (000) 000-0000 and 000 000 0000, or 0000000000, or 000.000.0000. (Talk to your developers about this.)

Giving users an example of the input you expect can also reduce errors. It can be directly in a text field, for example, or part of your instructions.

When users miss a question or make a mistake, you should alert them so they can fix it. If it is a question that you can verify, you can show a check mark or an "X" to indicate whether it is correct or incorrect. This is called *inline error handling*. Password fields also use the inline method to indicate if the password is weak or strong as you type.

Do not use inline error handling if you can't verify the input, like when people type their name (i.e., you never know if a name is "correct.")

When the user clicks "next" or "done," you can check the form for missed questions or mistakes. If there is a problem, make it visually obvious which ones they missed and why they are wrong.

PROTIP

Make sure the user can see the error from the bottom of the form! If they have to scroll up to find out what happened, they won't.

Speed versus Mistakes

This is a little advanced, but *super* useful:

Are you asking really common questions like "name" and "email," or more unusual ones like "what's your favorite type of velvet artwork?"

For common questions, a form with labels that are left-aligned and above the input will get users through it as fast as possible. It keeps everything on the Axis of Interaction. For uncommon or complex questions, a form with labels to the left of the input (on the same row) will slow users down a little, but result in fewer errors.

For most forms, put the "done" button on the left, on the Axis of Interaction. If the form will do something really destructive or critical, put it on the right so people pause to look for it instead of clicking it by reflex.

Phew, that was a lot for one lesson! Good work!

Primary and Secondary Buttons

Users can click or tap many things in your design. Some of those actions are helpful to your goals, and some aren't.

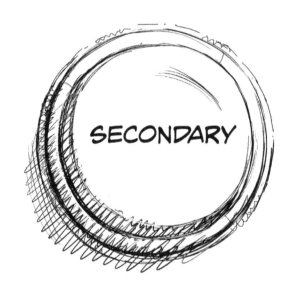

This example shows two button examples (don't tap them). As a general guideline, you will need only two button styles because most user actions fall into one of two categories:

1. Primary Actions that are helpful to our goals.

2. Secondary Actions that are not.

Primary Buttons

Some actions that are available to the user are productive, like registering, buying, submitting content, saving, sending, sharing, and so on. They produce things that didn't exist before. Those are *primary actions*, or things that we want the user to do as often as possible.

Buttons that execute primary actions—primary buttons—should be as visible as possible. We do that by using the principles we learned earlier in the course.

Primary style
> High contrast compared to the background (very different color or shade).

Position in layout
> On or near the Axis of Interaction so users notice them first, by reflex.

Secondary Buttons

Some actions that are available to the user are counterproductive, like canceling, skipping, resetting, declining an offer, and so on. They remove or stop the creation of new things. Those are secondary actions, or things we don't want the user to do, but we provide the option for the sake of usability.

Therefore, buttons that execute secondary options—secondary buttons—should be less visible, to prevent accidental or "reflexive" clicks.

Secondary style
> Low contrast compared to the background (a similar color or shade).

Position in layout
> Away from the Axis of Interaction so users notice them only when they are looking for them.

Importance Is a BIG Exception

Sometimes counterproductive actions are important, like deleting your account. Those actions should get *a primary style* but *secondary position* in the layout. The reason is that we want the user to find it, but we want them to think about their action before doing it. It is also a good idea to give this button a *warning* color that indicates the importance of the action (red, orange, yellow, etc.).

Special Buttons

In some cases, you will have one type of action that is unique to your site or app, which requires special focus. Design a special button for this so it stands out in your design (*pattern breaking*).

Amazon's "One-Click Purchase" buttons, Pinterest's "Pin it" button, and Facebook's good ol' thumbs-up "Like" button all got this treatment (more or less).

Adaptive and Responsive Design

UX is not one-size-fits-all, so you will eventually find yourself trying to fit your giant web design onto any number of other, smaller devices. Don't panic. Adapt.

Adaptive Design Is Really Just a Couple of Different Designs

A lot of beginner designers are confused between *adaptive* and *responsive* design terminology, but it's actually pretty simple.

Adaptive design is a few different designs; one for each of the device types you think are important. For example, if you have a webshop and you have customers visiting on mobile and desktop web, then you might design a small phone-sized version, and a bigger desktop version. If someone visits on a phone, they see the small one, and if they visit on a bigger screen, they see the big one.

That's it.

Adaptive design takes less time and it's easier because it is a lot more static than responsive design. Lots of designers will post a version of their design for mobile and a version for web and call it "responsive," but in reality they often haven't designed the "in between" states of the design.

Responsive Design Is One Design That Fits All Screens

Responsive design "stretches" and "adjusts" as you change the size of the window, so no matter what device you're using or what resolution your screen has, it works perfectly.

How does this magical responsiveness occur, you say? Well, it's all about "break points."

One layout can't stretch forever and still look good, so you have to decide when to show or hide some features and how far you want something to stretch before it will "break" and change to a layout that will show things better at that size. Then, when a device loads the page, or the window changes size, the site adjusts automatically, providing an orgasmically perfect experience to everybody.

There is no way to cover all the aspects of responsive design in a short lesson like this, but as you get deeper into UX, it is worth reading more about it.

To Design or Redesign?

It is only a matter of time before you have to choose between improving the thing that exists or creating something new.

Sometimes a new design from scratch is the obvious choice. Like when your company still uses its site from 1998, and that multicolored, animated unicorn background just doesn't say *professionalism* like it used to.

Sometimes an improvement to the old design is the obvious choice. Like when the designers update the brand accent color from a nice forest green to a fresh, minty green, but all the features stay the same.

No brainers.

But what about when the site is two years old, and several users have mentioned that Thing A and Thing B aren't quite as good as your competitors? Not so obvious.

Define the Problem First

If you don't know what you're solving, you don't know how to solve it. So, first, decide exactly what result you're aiming for, and think about how far your current design is from doing that.

If users are confused because they often overlook a button, you might be able to solve it by changing the button color. If users are confused because the structure of your site makes as much sense as Donald Trump's presidential campaign, then you might need a bigger change to solve the problem.

Make the Smallest Change You Can Make

Sometimes doing *everything* is simpler than doing *one thing*. When you have a sense of the problem and what it might take to solve that problem, don't look for the biggest, coolest way to solve it. Look for the minimum number of changes you can make that will get the job done.

For example, let's say your menu is confusing. If you can solve the problem by making the menu labels more clear, then do that. Changing text is easy to do and easy to test. If that isn't enough, maybe you can add some *cross-links* within the site so users can easily find what they want, even when they navigate to the wrong page. No problem.

Or, if that isn't enough, maybe you can redesign the home page so it provides obvious shortcuts to the popular stuff that is a bit hard to find.

Or, if that isn't enough, maybe you can move/combine a couple pages so they exist where the users expect to find them.

But…

If your code is really old or it's built on a shitty Content Management System, or if other big things need to be changed at the same time, or if your company wants to make money in a different way… all of the previously described redesigns might be *more difficult* than just throwing the whole site in the garbagio (that's Italian for garbage…probably) and starting from scratch.

A new design from scratch takes away all the baggage of the old design, but it means that you have to be more careful about using all of the existing data and managing expectations. If Facebook had a totally different design tomorrow, everybody would be pissed off, even if the new design is better. Either way, remember to help the users learn the new design!

Sometimes the Best Redesign Is Less

Adding features isn't always the right choice. It is always worth asking yourself if you can solve a problem by taking things *away*. Maybe your navigation is confusing because there are too many options that nobody cares about. Maybe you have given the users so much content that the page is hard to scan. Maybe you offer so many features that it's too much to learn, so nobody stays long enough to understand it!

And maybe you can automate a bunch of things to make the user's job simpler, even if that means making your job more complicated. When it comes to interfaces, less is usually more.

Touch versus Mouse

The psychology of any interface might be the same, but the practical details can be very different depending on what the device itself can do.

A Mouse Has Some Advantages Over a Finger

A mouse pointer (the little arrow) is an extension of your hand that lives on the screen, allowing you to interact with a bigger screen without even being near it.

Small and accurate

Since a mouse pointer isn't a physical "thing," it can be any size we want (in theory). In this case, smaller means more accurate. A mouse can actually select a single pixel, although one-pixel buttons are not recommended. But if you want to do something that requires fine control or lots of detail, like Photoshopping Justin Bieber in an underwear ad, then a mouse will perform better.

Ability to hover

A mouse pointer is like Samuel L. Jackson: always on screen. And the computer knows where it is. The best advantage of a mouse is that it can cause changes without clicking. When the user positions the pointer "over" a button or a menu (i.e., hovering), the interface can change color or reveal options that they didn't even know about—that's called *discovery*.

Selects items easily

A mouse can click small areas, between individual letters, or click-and-drag to select a specific area. This is also a big advantage over fingers, which block our view and scroll the screen when we "touch and drag." The mouse pointer, therefore, is much better (or faster) when it comes to working with text and image editing, which require careful selections, or when working with games that require precision.

Hidden options/navigation

Using the right mouse button (or a Cmd-click on Mac) in most software and some websites will display a menu or advanced options. This can allow you to design common shortcuts into the mouse pointer itself instead of showing them on the screen. And everything on the screen can have a different right-click menu. Some touch-based apps have a touch-and-hold concept that is similar, but it is slower and less obvious.

Can change shape

Unlike a finger, the mouse pointer can look like anything you want! An arrow, a hand, an icon, a cute little baby pig, and so on. When the cursor changes, it tells the user what will happen if the user clicks, like when the pointer becomes a hand over a link (a touch metaphor!). A lot of software takes advantage of this to provide rich visual feedback.

Your Finger Has Some Advantages Over a Mouse

Most people have 10 of these bad boys, and they have been designed by a natural process called evolution, which tends to be rather good at designing tools. Here are some of the benefits of your trusty ol' fingers:

Built-in feedback

Your fingers have nerves in them, which tell your brain when they touch something. When your finger is touching the screen, you don't need visual feedback to confirm it. That being said, visual feedback is still a good idea. In the very near future though, devices will probably give you haptic feedback that you can feel with your fingers!

Direct-to-interface

Instead of reaching for the mouse when you want to click the button, you reach for the button. That might sound small, but it means much less work for your brain.

Creates a physical orientation

The direct connection to your interface means people start assuming that a lot of real-world physical properties apply. Want to make something bigger? Stretch it. Smaller? Pinch it. Move it up? Put your finger on it and slide it up. You might not have realized that scrolling "down" on a screen means moving the content "up" in the real world. Touch devices change this, making "up" mean up and "down" mean down.

Always available

On a touch screen you type and click and select with the same thing: your finger! You also know where your finger is when you're not using it, so it never gets lost. Hopefully.

Gestures and multitouch

Gesturing with your hands is part of every conversation ever (assuming you have functional hands), so when we have to do a swipe or pinch, it's no problem. Sometimes we have to teach people what gesture to use, though, so be careful about using crazy or complicated ones. If you need to do something a little more complex, a better choice might be a *multitouch* gesture, which is when you use more than one finger.

Fully trained right out of the box

By the time you're about four years old, you have conquered the basics of motor skills, and that is proven by the fact that little kids can use an iPhone just as well as some adults. If you watch those same kids use a mouse you will notice that it is less comfortable, and they might look at the mouse sometimes to stay oriented.

X

Psychology of Usability

What Is Usability, Really?

Your design will affect how much the user must think to get the job done. If you made a scale that goes from "no thinking" to "thinking hard," that would be a usability scale.

One of the most common myths in UX is that good usability is more pleasing to the eye.

It is impossible for something to "look usable." If someone says that about your design, ignore it.

When users are surveyed about which design is "most usable," their opinions are more related to the beauty than the effectiveness. This means we can't trust user opinions about how usable a design is.

Usability is measured by what people *do*:

- If more people buy something in an uglier design, it is more usable.
- If people read more in an uglier design, it is more usable.
- If more people register via the uglier design, it is more usable.

Sometimes you will be forced to choose between beauty and usability. Always choose usability.

Usability = Cognitive Load

Cognitive load is the amount of processing power that is required to complete any little thing we make a user's brain do. For example:

- It takes less work to continue what you're doing than to do something different.
- It takes less work to find something again than it did to find it the first time.
- It takes less work to read simple words than to read complicated words.
- It takes less work to agree than it does to complain.

Every detail in your design (and in your life) should reduce the amount of cognitive load between the user (or yourself) and positive goals.

Usability is every detail, every moment, every time.

Don't Ignore Beauty!

Beauty is not irrelevant in UX. It is easy and fast to decide that you like the way something looks. That can lead to quick downloads, instant trust, and more persuasive designs. Beauty cannot make something more usable, but it can make users *feel* like it is more usable, and that is important, too.

In UX, your job is to test, measure, and research that beauty, not to create it.

Over the next few lessons you will learn some of the psychological factors that increase usability but might not affect the way something looks to an outsider.

AS A UX DESIGNER

It is your job to use psychology—and confirm it with tests—even if it makes something a little uglier. That being said, don't do anything because it's ugly. That's just dumb. Ugliness doesn't guarantee usability either.

ONLY YOU, CAN PREVENT SHITTY INTERFACES.

Simple, Easy, Fast, or Minimal

UX designers are always trying to make functions better and nicer for the user. But in different situations, that means different approaches. So let's compare four different ways of thinking about usability.

A word you might hear in UX is: heuristics. A *heuristic* is an approach or a strategy for solving a problem. Let's say you want to get more people to finish a process with many steps. Like a checkout, or a registration, or getting through the body-scanners at the airport.

(i.e., You want to increase conversion.)

Below are four ways you could think about it (heuristics), each with their own advantages and disadvantages.

Simpler: Fewer Steps

It's only a matter of time, as a UX designer, before someone brings you a seven-page registration flow that needs to be simplified.

You could:

- Remove any questions that aren't necessary, like confirming your email address.

- Detect information, like the type of credit card, instead of asking for it.

- Automatically format answers properly, like a phone number, instead of asking for it in several chunks (or using errors).

The disadvantage with simplification is that it might collect less information or take more time to build. And if you don't confirm that email address, a typo can ruin the whole registration.

Easier: More Obvious Steps

It is almost always possible to make a question more obvious. Just pretend you're designing for one of the guys from Duck Dynasty.

You could:

- Let them choose their country from a list instead of asking them to type it.

- Add super-clear instructions for every question, including questions like "Your name."
- Break complex questions into more steps so each step is easier to understand.

The disadvantage with making things more obvious is that it often creates more questions or more reading for the user, which works against your simplification.

Faster: Less Time to Complete/ Repeat the Process

Often, the process itself is something the user has done many times before, or they will do it many times in the future. Over time, making it faster can improve your conversion a lot.

You could:

- Let them save their address and autocomplete it for them next time.
- Choose popular defaults so most people don't have to change anything.
- Make shortcuts like Amazon's one-click purchase for people who are logged in.

The disadvantage with designing for speed is that you make the process less flexible—changes mean slowing down—and mistakes are easy to overlook while you're click, click, clicking your way to the end.

Minimal: Fewer Functions

Many designers believe minimalism is about flat design, or hiding your options in a hidden menu. It definitely is *not*.

Minimalism is about doing less, better. In theory, minimalism makes a design simpler, easier, *and* faster. For example, Outlook is an email app with a lot of features like an address book, a full-featured calendar, meeting reminders, and different ways to sort your inbox. It is not minimal. It may be more powerful, but it is also harder to learn.

Sparrow, on the other hand, is an email app that allows you to send, receive, forward, delete, and put emails in folders— and that's basically it. It is very popular and easier to learn but not as powerful.

Minimalism often requires a redesign from the ground up, and although it makes the fundamentals of your product better, it might not be enough for power users.

A Mix of Strategies Is Usually Best

To choose heuristics that are best for you, interview users to learn about their mental strategies, ask the "stakeholders" in your company about their needs, and always A/B–test your choices to confirm that they are better.

Browsing, Searching, or Discovery

Different people use sites and apps for different reasons. If you design for the wrong behavior, you won't get the results you want.

This can mean a variety of things in the real world, so for the purposes of this lesson, let's clarify:

Browsing

> This is when you go to Ikea to look at all the model rooms "just to get ideas," and you probably walk out with a bunch of random crap anyway.

Searching

> Searching is when you go to Ikea looking for a new sofa that will fit in your absurdly small apartment.

Discovery

> This is when you find the sofa you're looking for and also buy the clever little nested end-tables from the same showroom, because they are so damn clever and nested. As if those are things you need in your life.

Browsing

When you visit an online store just because their products look nice or because you're following trends, or because you're dreaming of the day when your life will finally be completed by a $2,000 watch, you are browsing.

A browsing user will glance quickly at most of the images, one by one, starting at the upper left. She might skip some, but that's ok. Photos that the user finds attractive will get extra attention (maybe even a click!).

To design for browsing: Make scanning easy and keep the content quick and visual. Don't overcrowd the page with too much shit. Focus on the aspects of the products that create emotional appeal. If that's style, focus on photos. If that is power (like boat engines or guns) then provide that info as clear labels. If that is brand names, clearly show the logos. If it is craftsmanship, magnify the handcrafted details. And so on.

Searching

When someone is trying to find something they have in mind, it might seem similar to browsing, but eye-tracking studies show a very different behavior: they are hunting. A searching user will ignore a lot of products or pictures. Organization in your layout will help them systematically work through the options; they don't want to miss any! A Pinterest-style layout works against them because it is "staggered" and random. But being able to "filter" the options is often useful.

To design for searching: Focus on attributes. If users want a restaurant with a certain price range and style, they will stop at every option that seems to have those qualities. Highlight the attributes that are most likely to be "critical" for most users, and nothing more. Ignore any ideas you might have about what looks "cluttered"; if the information is useful, it isn't "clutter." This isn't an art gallery.

When the user finds what they want, they will click for more information (or buy). A restaurant's menu, photos, and prices might be major points of interest, but the number of seats or name of the sous-chef, not so much.

Discovery

Ok, so let's say your users aren't finding your amazing selection of antique kazoos, but you think they would buy them if they did. How do you create discovery? The way you think people discover new things is probably the opposite of how people actually discover new things. Welcome to the wacky world of UX.

There are two mistakes you will probably make:

1. You will put it in the main menu or create "banners" on your own site promoting it.

2. You will expect your most loyal users to find it first because they spend the most time with your current design.

Both of those things are wrong.

Mistake 1: Users only click things in the menu if they are looking for those things. Simple as that. Almost nobody "discovers" via the menu. And banners don't work because banners never work. Haven't you ever used the Internet before? Why would people suddenly get excited about banners now?

Mistake 2: The more experienced a user is, the less they explore for new things. In real life, only beginners explore sites or apps to find out what it can do. Experienced users know what they want and they know how to get it, so why would they explore?

"If you liked that, you're gonna love this…"

Instead of relying on users to find new things, let them find what they are already looking for. Put the new stuff there, too, (and make it relevant) so they can "discover" it. This might feel like you're hiding it, but really you're making it as visible as possible to the right people.

On a site like Reddit, people come for the top-voted content, not new submissions. But if nobody votes on new submissions, there will be no top-voted content! So, Reddit puts a few new submissions—from the categories you like—into the top content so they become visible, get votes, and start the Circle of Life once again.

The more you understand your users, the more you will know what to design for. Do your damn research!

Consistency and Expectations

Consistency is a way to make learning faster and create useful expectations about what comes next. But consistency is not automatically good design.

Consistency is the idea that a design looks the same from page to page, or device to device, or user to user. And in general, it's a good thing. When I log in this time, I expect a site or an app to be the same as last time. It helps me find the menu, navigate to things I like, and quickly skip the advertising at the beginning. Branding-wise, it also helps me recognize the company, trust the content, and know that I came to the right place.

Patterns Require Consistency

A brain is a pattern-recognition machine. It is designed to experience something once, and then be better at doing the same thing again. That is why the menu should be in the same place on every page and screen, colors should indicate warnings and importance the same way everywhere, and why next time you will *not* ignore the sock on the doorknob of your parents' room.

Consistency creates expectations. When the user expects something to work a certain way, and it does, that's good usability.

But…

Consistency Is a Tool, Not a Rule

If someone slaps you in the face, you will flinch the next time she raises her hand. You expect her to do it again. If you want the user to expect the same thing, design it the same way. But often you don't want that.

Your app and your website do not have to look exactly the same. You click one and swipe the other; differences can communicate that difference. One user is very unlikely to use your app on an Android phone and an iPhone at the same time, for example, so if the features of those devices use *slightly* different approaches, fine! After all, the devices are *slightly* different.

A landing page, a home page, and a check-out have different goals, so don't worry that they look a bit different. They should!

Anti-UX

We are always trying to help our users, but that doesn't always mean agreeing with them. And it would be naïve not to realize that we have the power to deceive users with UX techniques.

There is a difference between a bad UX design, and a UX design that works against the user. The difference is psychology. Anti-UX prevents mistakes and bad decisions by using normal UX principles, in the opposite direction.

The Good, The Bad, and The Anti

Let's say you run a members-only website for clown car mechanics. It's a lot of great content on one tiny site.

Members pay a subscription each month, until they cancel it. The price might look small, but you get so much out of it!

You don't want people to cancel their account, obviously, but it is necessary to allow it, obviously. Otherwise, they all might repaint their faces with a single tear and a frowny mouth.

Let's say we're designing that cancellation process.

Good UX

The form should be clear and easy. The "cancel my subscription" button should be somewhere logical (like account settings). You should get an email to confirm the cancellation. Everything should be easy to read, relevant, and so on.

Bad UX

If you are an unethical designer—which I hate—then you could make the form difficult and confusing. You could hide the "cancel" button somewhere weird or make it tiny and hard to see. And it could "fail" when the user makes a tiny mistake, so they have to start from the beginning.

The problem

In real life, bad UX will create fewer cancellations than good UX, which is better for the company.

Uh oh. *More* money for a *worse* experience? That's not good.

However, there is a solution…

Anti-UX

Everything from the "good UX" example remains the same. Clear and easy. But we're also going to throw in some psychology to fix "the problem."

If your marketing department wants to know why the user is cancelling, put it in the form. A bunch of boring questions is a great way to reduce conversion. Break the form into several pages so it takes longer. Include links to FAQ pages that might "help" the user leave the cancellation process. And avoid using defaults; it maximizes the number of conscious choices for the user.

These things are all easy to do, but they all make you think rationally and they take time.

Show the user an article they loved, like "10 Ways to Stuff More Clowns into a Selfie," or pictures of their best clown friends, or offer exclusive access to the Big Red Shoes Club (you know what they say about people with big red shoes!).

(i.e., Remind the user what they will *lose* by cancelling.)

Nothing should be difficult or deceptive. We're not trying to stop the user. We're trying to remove the emotional motivation to cancel, so they *choose* to stay. If they have a rational reason for leaving, they will still leave. And that's fine.

Dirty UX Tricks Hurt Us All

RyanAir is a discount European airline that used to have one of the most deceptive websites that I have ever seen.

The new site (as of this writing) is better, but still includes a default to pay for extra insurance you don't need. To unselect it, you scroll half way down a list of countries and pick "don't insure me" from the list. It doesn't make sense and it costs you money if you don't understand.

That's how you kill trust.

"Don't do that shit. Ever."

—R. McDonald, senior VP of clowns

Accessibility

When your projects will be used by the general public or specific groups of people who are very old, very young, hearing- or vision-impaired, who might not understand the languages you provide, etc., it's time to adjust your approach.

Accessibility is the idea of designing for people who have less-than-typical abilities in one way or another. Not necessarily a disability. Anything that could make a typical design hard to use in any way might fall under the category of accessibility. It is also one of those topics that could be—and probably is—a whole book of its own. So think of this as a very general overview.

For beginners, I think the main thing is that you know about accessibility and include it whenever you can.

Accessibility is a major consideration for *general public* sites like governments and universities, but also for any site with millions of users, like Facebook, Tumblr, news sites, etc.

Accessibility Is Visual

The simplest and most obvious way to make your designs more accessible is to make it easier to look at. This is actually very similar to the idea of designing for different devices, except that the differences are the users instead of the device.

Big text is easier to read, so if your audience is a little older or visually impaired, spend some extra time on readability. Color blindness is a real thing, and more common than you might think. Depending on your audience, up to 10% of them might have trouble with red and green, for example, so they might not be the best combination for "yes" and "no" options.

Accessibility Is Technology

Did you know that sight-impaired people use software called Screen Readers to read everything on the Internet? That software will often read everything in the order it is laid out in the code, so it is worth making sure that is done properly. Screen readers might also read content in the "tab order"—the order you will select the content if you just hit the Tab key over and over—so if you want users with poor or no vision to get to the good stuff quickly, consider that detail.

Accessibility Is Content

Use simple words, simpler grammar, so people who are not-so-great in your language can still read without a lot of trouble.

Make it easy to change the language. Many sites—especially American ones—forget that two-thirds of the world doesn't speak English very well. For many users, the language selector is not a minor detail; it is a make-or-break feature.

Make the content shorter so it doesn't take as long to listen to it. Make it easy to jump within long pages. Make it easy to scan.

Accessibility Is Extra Thoughtful

Like all things in UX, you should try using an app or the Internet like your audience will. I promise you this: about 30 seconds into your testing, you will hate yourself and every other designer who hasn't considered these things.

But don't stop there! Really think about your design instead of just *looking* at it. What would you want if you were 80 years old, not tech-savvy, and just needed to find a recipe online because you can't remember anything for more than a few minutes?

XI

Content

UX Copywriting versus Brand Copywriting

When it comes to copywriting, UX people and true copywriters care about different things. Our focus is on specific types of writing, and we're not in it for the poetic street cred.

Copywriting in UX Is Usability

Remember when I said that the purpose of UX is to make the user *effective*, not happy? Copywriting is probably the most pure example of that. Perfect UX copy is understood immediately and forgotten after it serves its purpose.

The UX designer is not the copywriter, or the marketer, or the salesperson, or the creative director. So, when we write copy we need to focus on making the user *understand and engage*.

Our headlines are calls-to-action, not storytelling.

Our explanations are instructional, not inspirational.

Our form labels are simple, not clever.

And our buttons labels are written for clarity, not to maximize whitespace.

Copywriting in Branding Should Create Associations

Remember when we learned about memory? Humans connect certain things with certain feelings. The goal of *brand* copywriting is to create those associations.

You might want users to believe your company is more *human* or more *scientific* or more *authentic* than your competitors, and the way to make them think that is to *write in a certain tone*.

A brand copywriter might write a clever tagline or campaign slogan like Nike's "Just Do It." They might write headlines so they feel more fun, like MailChimp's quirky copy. They might name products or features to make them more "catchy" or "on brand" like Apple's iEverything or McDonald's McEverything or Ben & Jerry's flavor names.

Work Together!

These might seem like opposite things that could never work together, but that isn't true at all! UX and copywriting have the same ultimate goal: persuasion.

In UX we make things clear and simple so more people can get shit done. Brand copywriters make things more motivational so more people want to get shit done. But, UX strategy can make prices look more attractive. Brand copywriting can increase engagement. Brand copy can *motivate* users, which increases engagement. And UX makes products more *usable* which improves the users' impression of the brand.

In a perfect world, you want both.

Choose Your Battles

If someone is designing a beautiful ad with a five-word tagline for a fancy magazine, that's probably not the time for UX. If the text is readable, you're done unless there is a chance to do some eye-tracking. Let the copywriter do their thing.

(P.S.—Yes, I just used an offline example in a UX book. You didn't think UX happened only on the Internet, did you? UX happens in your mind, not on the screen.)

If you're designing a complex form that is critical to the success of the business and the copywriter wants the labels to be more poetic, tell them to go suck a lemon. A big one. UX can be gangsta like that sometimes.

Good usability is always *on brand*. Don't sacrifice function for style, ever.

The Call-To-Action Formula

Tiny changes in copy can make huge differences in results. The more important a button is, the more you should consider the details.

You can follow this formula for text on anything you want people to click:

Verb + Benefit + Urgent Time/Place

I have personally increased clicks on a button by 400% just by changing the text, and let me tell you: if you want your boss to think you're a wizard, this is the lesson for you.

Verb

The verb is the action word: get, buy, see, try, upgrade, download, register, win, lose… whatever. This should be first, because it gets to the point immediately and turns the button into a command.

Benefit

Sometimes the verb and the benefit are the same thing, like the word "upgrade"; it is both the action and the benefit. But in a phrase like "Download Version 2 Now!" the new version is the benefit. In the phrase "Lose 5 kilograms today!" the benefit is losing five kilograms. You get the idea. Just make sure the benefit is a benefit to the user, not the website. A phrase like "Become a Member" has no clear benefit for the user, but the person who owns the site thinks it sounds great.

Urgent Time or Place

Words like "now," "today," or "in 1 minute!" provide a time frame that is urgent and feels easy. Words like "here" or "this" tell users that the button itself is what they are looking for. "Like This" or "Start Here" are common examples.

On a button that says "Start Here!" you get an action, a benefit, and a place. In my experience, "Start Here" buttons work really well when the first question from a user will be "Where do I start?" Seems obvious, but it's not as obvious when you're planning the site in real life. In this case "here" describes the button itself.

Wild Card

The word "free" can sometimes take the place of an urgent time or place. If the button provides something big for the user like software, the user might assume there is a cost involved. In that case the word "free" can help reduce anxiety and improve click-through-rates. But use it carefully, it can also make premium brands feel less premium and imply that the benefit isn't worth much.

Things to Avoid

A Call-To-Action (CTA) button/link—the one that you want users to click, like a buy/register button—should never begin with "Click here to…" The fact that it is a button or a link has already told the user that they need to click it (if you designed it properly), you don't have to tell them again. That type of copy loses clicks because the user doesn't see the action or benefit that the button executes, so they don't click. "Click here to win" is not as good as "Win today!"

Also, long or difficult words on a button lose clicks. "Start here" would work much better than "Commence Forthwith" or "If you would like to enter the site begin by clicking this button." Silly examples, but it's important to remember.

Instructions, Labels and Buttons

AS A UX DESIGNER

It is your job to help users complete tasks properly, and that often means telling them what something is, and what they should do with it.

If it isn't 100% obvious how users should do something—and even if it is—you might want to help them out.

Instructions should be short, literal, and direct. No lingo. No industry terms. No clever jokes or sarcasm or funny business. Don't be too wordy or too soft. Tell the users exactly what to do. Use the simplest words and phrases you know. Write to everyone as if they were smart children or a non-native speaker of the language. Not stupid, just clear. Here are some examples:

- **Bad:** "Swing on down to the clicky spot when yer all set!"

- **Also bad:** "All input in this area is required data and must be successfully submitted to initiate the account creation process."

- **Stupid:** "Look at you! You're so good at forms! When you get everything typed in there like a good form fill-er-outer, then you should just go ahead and click that fancy yellow button below! You're almost there, champ!"

- **Good:** "Answer every question. When you're finished, click the yellow *Done* button at the bottom of this page."

Labels

It can be very tempting to make labels clever or unique, but always resist that temptation. Use the most common, easiest, most basic version of the label that you can imagine. If your label can have more than one type of answer, it might not be clear enough yet. Take a look at these:

- **Bad:** "Where your heart is…"

- **Not good:** "The place where you live"

- **Better:** "Address"

- **Best:** "Home Address"

Labels also apply to buttons, which is something that a lot of designers overlook.

If you skip the headline and the instructions, will you still understand what the buttons do? If not, make the labels better.

- **Bad Button Labels:** "Ok" or "Yes"
- **Good Button Labels:** "Ignore Changes" or "Save Changes"

However, this is one of the times in UX when the method is fairly easy and the real-life scenario can get political. If you have a creative director or a copywriter or client looking at your text and saying, "We need to make it more awesome," you should say no.

Prove it with an A/B test if you must, but never back down when the text is for practical, functional reasons. Sometimes, the "experience" the user needs is something simple and clear, not something awesome and confusing.

Landing Pages

The first page a user sees when they arrive on your site for the first time has one job: get them in the door.

Think About Your Site or App Like an Airport

You have never been to this city, and you're arriving from somewhere else in the world. You get off the plane with your (emotional) baggage and your first question is always the same:

"Where do I go?"

You might want to find a taxi, or a toilet, or some food, but it's usually something like that, and you will go for the first thing that looks like it will meet your needs.

The difference with a landing page on your website is that people can decide to get back on the plane. Your job is to show people where to go so they don't get back on the plane.

A good landing page answers the *Three Whats of UX*:

1. What is this?
2. What's in it for me?
3. What should I do next?

Three Whats = One job

A landing page should be so focused that you don't even need the main menu. In fact, the menu often makes a landing page *less effective* because it distracts the user.

Maybe they want to know how your site works and how to sign up. Maybe your campaign made them curious and they want to know more. Maybe you're selling to other businesses and they need to see if your product fits their budget and needs. Maybe a friend recommended your product and that's all they know!

If you understand what your users want, you should be able to tell them exactly why they are in the right place and how to get what they want.

Your Site Can Have *Many* Landing Pages

One of them will probably be the "home" page, but that's not the only one. Don't make the mistake of assuming that every user will come in the front door.

It's a good idea to create landing pages for your campaigns, common Google searches, and for any other specific source of traffic that you expect/get. The job of these landing pages is to create interest. You measure interest by whether the user *clicks something or not.*

Landing Pages Are Important

When a new user *doesn't* click anything on your landing pages, that's called a *bounce.* A user who bounces cannot do anything else with your site/app/product, because they are gone.

They can't register, or buy, or share, or post content. You are *failing* to make them a user at all.

Therefore, any time you spend optimizing a landing page is time well spent. Even a 1% improvement could mean thousands or millions of dollars in sales, depending on what you're working on. On the other hand, if 80% of the visitors fail to "land," your airport has an emergency on its hands.

Readability

If you were some other kind of designer, this lesson might be called *Typography*. But since you're a UX designer, let's talk about how you should treat type for maximum effectiveness.

Forget About Choosing Serif or Sans Serif

In UX, you don't care. Even Comic Sans is acceptable, technically, although I wouldn't fight for it if I were you.

Readability is the word for the "usability" of big blocks of text. Long Wikipedia articles, lists of Google search results, your manifesto about miniature donkeys—that sort of thing.

When other kinds of designers are looking at fonts and typography, they should be choosing what *tone* and *style* those typefaces create in the design. They obviously want people to be able to read the text, as well, but it isn't necessarily the first concern.

On a bottle of Absolut Vodka, for example, the fancy script is a little hard to read, but it looks "fancy," which is what the designer wanted most. A UX designer would have had a panic attack about the idea of writing a whole paragraph in that script, but they did it anyway, because readability wasn't their main concern.

On the other hand, if you are a news site, writing your articles in a fancy script is probably a great way to get death threats and go bankrupt.

That's where UX comes in.

Readability Is a Combination of Things

Depending on your design, various things might help. The person doing the typography will be a great resource, as well, since they spend a lot of their time playing with text.

Here are some things to try:

Is the text big enough?

Small text tends to look better but it's difficult to read, especially on mobile devices. Try increasing the size of all the text in general. That's also a good way to make it *feel* simpler.

Add space between the letters

This is called *kerning* or *tracking*. When letters get a little too close together, they can become hard to read, especially in a paragraph. Put some "air" in there to make it easier to read.

Add space between the lines

This is called *leading.* As a general rule, the space between the lines should be about 1.5 times the height of one line of text. More can be nice, too. Don't add too much though, or else it might be too distracting to go from one line to the next.

Add space around the text

All the other crap in your design might be distracting people from reading. That's why "reader mode" in some browsers and apps take away everything except the text. Focus.

Adjust the width of the column

The optimal width for a column is said to be between 45 and 75 characters, give or take. The narrower end (50-ish) *feels* better, and the wider end (70-ish) is actually faster. You can adapt your design based on the device and the type of content.

Use real content, and actually *read it*

If you're trying to do any of this with *lorem ipsum* dummy text, then you're not really doing UX. You can only test *readability* by using text that is *readable.* Even better, try copying and pasting an article that you actually want to read!

The Persuasion Formula

Forcing users to do things is usually a bad idea. People don't like being forced. Instead, we must convince them to take action, and the process of "convincing" tends to follow a simple eight-step formula.

> **NOTE**
> Persuasion is complex. My book, *The Composite Persuasion*, is 270 pages specifically about making things persuasive, and it is only a "Crash Course"!

The Persuasion Formula

After comparing 40 different types of persuaders, I found that all of their methods share 8 common attributes, listed below.

Before the Interaction

Credibility

Without trust, everything else is irrelevant. Ideally you should build your credibility for real; however, the main thing is to communicate with others in a high-value way. In UX, this applies to everything from trustworthy branding, to transparency about your prices, to testimonies from customers. Don't say you're valuable; show that value to your users.

Know your audience

In UX, that means you do your user research so you know who you are persuading and what they care about.

During the Interaction

Open and disarm

You have to engage the user's interest immediately and then proceed to remove any obvious objections they might have. In UX, this can be a great headline or an eye-catching image above the fold. If price is a concern, for example, that should be part of the first information the user can see. Don't assume they will continue far enough to learn about it later.

Create rapport

(Say *rah-por*) is the feeling of getting along with someone and it is created by similarities between people. In UX, this can be created by using familiar language, showing what the user has in common with your customers, or describing the main person in your article in a way that makes the reader relate to them.

Isolate

When a user has come far enough that their interest is clear, you want to remove any competing information. In UX, that might mean removing the menu or banners during the checkout process so nothing distracts the user from their purchase.

Convince

For more complex persuasions, you might need to provide "waves" of information that leads the customer from the basics to the details, so they understand step-by-step. There are a variety of ways to do this. Cognitive biases are often helpful to frame the information in a way that makes it easier to accept, and easier to consume.

Close the deal

Just ask for commitment and don't overcomplicate it. In UX this is the "publish" button or the "confirm purchase" button, or the "share" button.

After the Interaction

Summarize with bias

Don't let the persuasion end with the close! That makes people feel like you only value them until they give you what you want. In UX, this might be a follow-up email to remind them about everything they can do with their new Macbook, or suggestions for more articles, or feedback about how many people liked/agreed with their post.

How to Motivate People to Share

It is possible to make exactly the same idea engaging or boring just by the way you present it. More important, you can motivate people to contribute, comment, and share by making their contribution a source of pride.

Imagine someone posts in a forum and asks, "How do I get laid?" At first glance, you're not particularly interested in helping, unless you fancy yourself an artist with this sort of thing. This is the way a lot of corporations approach their social media activities; direct questions and factual posts, and self-centered content. It doesn't create engagement.

Now imagine if it were phrased more like this: "What is the fastest you have ever had sex with someone after meeting them? How did it happen?" Suddenly the reader has been challenged to tell a story that makes them look good, or at least makes them interesting. There is no obvious benefit for the person asking the question, but that doesn't mean there is no benefit for them.

It's more fun to have a crappy or funny answer than not to answer, and that's the whole objective here. It creates engagement!

This version of the question was on the real-life front page of Reddit, with more than 700 comments. (One person answered "17 years." Clearly an artist.)

Another common example of this idea is when someone gets laughs for doing something embarrassing. They will, para-doxically, do it again and again to get more laughs and more attention. (Conditioning!) The same effect would be achieved if you asked people "what is the worst rejection you have ever received?" This type of question on Reddit often includes the original person (the one who is asking) giving their own example first.

Now the rewards have been set so the worst story wins, so embarrassing yourself gains status, and everybody wants to be the worst! Much more effective than "*Is it normal to be rejected like this?*"

Instead of asking for help or examples directly, ask for examples of greatness. Or create an environment where horrible failure is desired by all.

Instead of just telling people to continue or share or click, motivate them with a teaser headline, cliff-hanger, or the promise of a reward or an opportunity.

If you're a brand on social media, you will create a reason for a lot of people to spend a lot of time with you, building good feelings about your brand the whole time. Just don't fall into the trap of clickbait. If you have shitty content, everyone will be disappointed when they get to it, and then your site or company will be associated with disappointment. Not good.

XII

The Moment of Truth

The Launch Is an Experiment

The main difference between UX design and other types of design is that we can measure our designs to see if they work. And we do that using the *scientific method*.

It is normal to think of the launch as the end of the creative process. But don't.

That process is uncertain: strategic decisions are just educated predictions. Design is a matter of taste; people make irrational decisions all the time. The only way to *know* is to do some science, and good science always needs a question, a hypothesis, an experiment, results, and interpretation.

Or what we in the industry like to call…

The Scientific Method

The Question/Problem

First and always, you need to start with a question. In your case, it might be a user problem. Your job is to understand the problem well enough that you can describe it specifically and then design a way to solve it.

Many people think that you should come up with some questions first and then use UX research to *answer* the questions,

but that's wrong. That's called guessing. UX research is supposed to *find* the questions and problems. By researching users and data you will uncover user behavior that needs to be fixed, or doesn't make sense. Why do users do that weird thing? What is the main problem for the user? How do users think about this feature? Why do people leave on the second step of the checkout? Why do so many people *bounce* on our landing page?

There are millions of those questions.

Hypothesis

Your design is your hypothesis: a strategy to solve the problem or answer the question. It is based on your research and data. It is your solution to the problem or question that you discovered in your research. You think it will work because the evidence says it will work.

The problem in digital projects is that you are usually so busy celebrating your launches that you forget to see if they actually *work*. UX is not a matter of taste, it is a matter of *results*. Just because you like it, doesn't mean it's good.

Prediction

Before you design your experiment, you should make a prediction about what will change if you are right about your hypothesis. That means you need to decide how you will measure that change.

If you think people don't notice the button because it is the wrong color, what will change when you fix that problem? What will you measure to know if it worked?

If you think people aren't engaged because you need more unicorns and rainbows, what will change when you fix that problem? What will you measure to know if it worked?

Experiment

Change your attitude: The launch is the *experiment*, not the result. You don't *know* anything until you *prove it* with *real* users. If you have done your research well and based your design on that research, you're not guessing. You're *experimenting*. Big difference.

Results

After you launch a site, you can get results like how long people stay on your site or how many registered or bought. These are not guesses, they are facts. You might need to wait a month or two on a small site, but the data will come.

These facts might not agree with your strategy. They might indicate that your design—although beautiful—is confusing. And they might prove that your obnoxiously large logo is distracting.

This is not a failure or a weakness; it is part of launching a site professionally. There are some things we just can't know before launching. The site might also be humankind's greatest creation, but we don't know that, either, until we test it in the real world.

XIII

Data for Designers

Can You Measure a Soul?

One common opinion in UX is the idea that you can't measure feelings. That isn't actually true, especially when we measure the feelings of a group.

A soul?!

Ok, ok… it may sound religious, but I am referring to the emotional, subjective parts of the human experience.

The soaring highs, the heartbreaking lows.

Call it whatever you want. It's who we are.

Point is: can we measure it? Yes we can!

Feelings produce actions and decisions, and those things can be measured pretty easily.

Neuromarketing

In UX, we usually don't have an fMRI machine in the office, but just as an example: there is an *emerging industry* that measures brains to discover which version of an ad or a movie creates the strongest emotions.

It's essentially an *A/B test*, (you will learn more about A/B tests in Lesson 95) with much cooler data than we usually get. When you do an A/B test, you are doing the same thing, but using actions instead of brain scans as your evidence.

Groups Are Reliable; Individuals, Not So Much

As we learned in Lessons 16–21, motivations (feelings) make people do stuff. Actions.

You might "Like" a photo, retweet an article, or embarrass yourself in front of millions of people because 50 people said you should try to swallow a spoonful of cinnamon.

In UX, our goal is to create actions, not just feelings. We motivate people so they will act in a certain way, which is helpful for everyone (including us).

When we measure individual people, we have to ask them face-to-face; otherwise, the details have too much influence to be reliable. A user might act differently because of the news this morning, or their personal interests, or because they are killing time on the toilet at work.

When you put a few thousand or a few million people in a group, however, those individual differences don't matter. The soul of the group becomes clear in the data.

When we talk about "the average person," we don't mean a specific person. We're talking about numbers. And those numbers measure the affect of your designs.

What Are Analytics?

Now that you have learned to research users, set goals, plan Information Architecture (IA), direct the users' attention, make good wireframes, and create usable features, it's time to launch! And launching means we have something to measure.

Data Is Objective

In one of the early lessons, we learned about user research.

Data is different.

Data measures user behavior. What they do, how many times they did it, how long it took, and so on.

It is collected by a computer, so it can't influence the user. It has well-defined measurements, so there is a very low margin of error. It can measure millions of people with no effort from you. And it can tell you things about your users like which browser they use or which country they are in.

And data never lies. This is science!

But it also doesn't tell you anything about context, so be careful. Unfortunately, we designers have to interpret the data, and that is where mistakes can happen.

Data Is Made of People

You will be tempted to treat data as "just numbers" that mean whatever you want them to mean. Remember that those numbers represent the actions of real people with complicated lives.

Do not reduce millions of people into a single number and expect it to be reliable in every situation.

You may also be tempted to look for numbers that "prove" you were right. DON'T. And say no to anyone who asks you for that.

More Data Is Better Data

If you measure the clicks of five people, they might all be drunk, and you have no way to know. If you measure the clicks of five million people, it's pretty unlikely that they are all drunk, unless you only test people in Cancun during Spring Break.

The bigger the decision you are trying to make with data, the more data you need before you decide. But once the data speak, the data have spoken!

A few ways to collect objective user data

There are just as many ways to get objective data as there are ways to get subjective user research:

Analytics

Google and many other companies offer cheap or free ways to track what your users do, anonymously. Basically, every time they load a page or click something, you will know. And you can design custom measurements, so the sky is the limit!

A/B tests

Design two versions of the same thing and launch both! You will know which one works better because you will test it with real people, in real time. The software also lets you know when to stop, because at a certain point, tracking more people isn't going to change much.

Eye-tracking

Special software and equipment are used to measure where the users look as they use your design, so you know where you have guided them well, or not. Eye movements are unconscious, so I consider eye-tracking objective.

Screen capture and heatmaps

Software like HotJar, ClickTale, and Lookback allow you to record the screens of real users while they use your product. Their input is hidden—everything is anonymous—but you see where they click, where the mouse goes, how far they scroll, and which pages they see as they move through your design. Some tools can also create "heatmaps" that use color to show you specifically where your users (as a group) clicked. Super useful.

Search logs

Many people don't realize that a search field on your site can save every word that is typed into it. If people are searching for it, it means they can't find it, so those logs are very valuable for improving your information architecture and layouts!

Graph Shapes

You don't need a deep knowledge of statistics to see interesting things in a graph. Human behavior makes a few basic shapes on a graph, and they all mean something.

There are two graph styles that human behavior creates fairly often: *Traffic* and *Structured Behavior*.

> **NOTE**
>
> I have used a bar graph in these examples because it was simpler to understand. Your analytics might use lines or dots or whatever. Don't panic. They all do basically the same thing. That's why we're learning shapes, not graph types.

Traffic Graphs

These graphs show the number of people that did something, over time. Like the number of visitors per day. You can call that "traffic."

Traffic will always be moving up and down a little because random things in the world happen every day, even when your site doesn't change at all.

That's why you can *never* assume that a small change in traffic was caused by a new feature or a design change.

Now, on with the shapes!

General Trend

If there is a slow consistent change, you will see it over time.

If it would be fairly easy to walk across your graph, and it shows a consistent "rise" or "fall," then the trend is likely to continue, unless you change it.

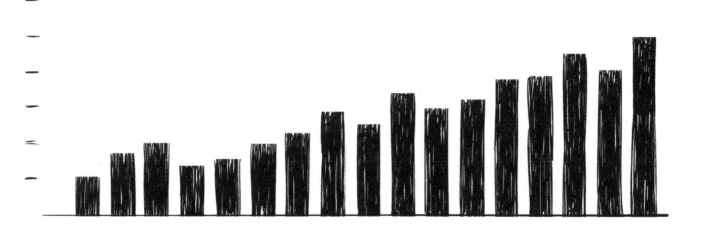

GENERAL TREND

IF THERE IS A SLOW, CONSISTENT CHANGE, YOU WILL SEE IT OVER TIME.

Random/Unexpected/One-time event

People don't suddenly change behavior without being provoked.

Did you run a weekend campaign? Or, is something technical causing problems on one of your pages? Or, maybe your startup just went public? When you see a spike in a graph (or a sudden drop), try to find out what is causing it, because—as tempting as it is to believe that you have spontaneously become cool—there is always a reason for a spike; sometimes good, sometimes bad.

RANDOM / UNEXPECTED /ONE-TIME EVENT

TEMPORARY BURST

PEOPLE DON'T SUDDENLY CHANGE BEHAVIOR WITHOUT BEING PROVOKED.

Predictable Traffic

A mature site (or a boring one) begins to have a clear pattern in visits.

See how there is a pattern repeating over and over, like a wave?

Sites that are popular with "office workers" often get more traffic during weekdays. If your users are all kids who go to school during the day, weekends might be your big days. That is very common and very normal.

But…

If it's a healthy pattern it will usually come with a slow growth trend, too. If you see a super-predictable pattern and your numbers are slowly going down, your users might be dying of boredom. Shake things up!

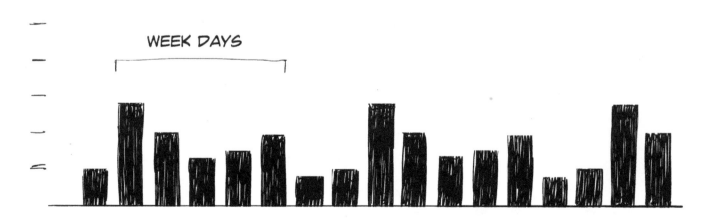

PREDICTABLE TRAFFIC

WEEK DAYS

A MATURE SITE (OR A BORING ONE) BEGINS TO HAVE A PATTERN IN VISITS.

Structured Behavior Graphs

The other big type of graph shows what people are doing. The date or hour when they did it isn't as relevant. You have a big effect on this type of behavior via your IA.

Exponential/Long Tail

This shows a strong bias toward a certain type of behavior or decision.

The graph shows a shape like a slide. More people will click the first thing than the second thing, and more people will click the second thing than the third thing. Any time there is a visual "order" or a natural sequence—like a menu that users read left to right—the graph will look like this.

EXPONENTIAL / LONG TAIL

THIS SHOWS A STRONG BIAS TOWARD A CERTAIN TYPE OF BEHAVIOR OR DECISION.

The list of "top pages" will usually look like this, too, because you can't get to page two without going through page one. The detailed view of Time-per-Visit or Pages-per-Visit (see Lesson 91 about time) also usually looks like this, because spending more than 10 seconds on a site is so damn difficult.

Exponential with Unexpected Order

When users are ignoring the structure you gave them, it looks like this.

This one is more interesting. If your data looks like it has all the right pieces but a few are in the wrong order, it means that users have different priorities than you thought. They are clicking the second thing before the first thing sometimes. Those crazy bastards!

Try to change your design/IA so it matches what the data is telling you. Don't try to change the users, though; they hate that.

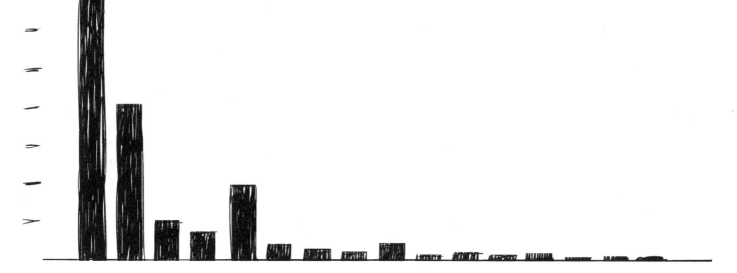

EXPONENTIAL WITH UNEXPECTED ORDER

WHEN USERS ARE IGNORING THE STRUCTURE YOU GAVE THEM, IT LOOKS LIKE THIS

Exponential with Power Users

This shows a small group of people who are doing a lot.

This graph looks pretty similar to the first "slide shape" but it has a bump. Some people think the graph is pregnant, but those people are idiots. This is what it looks like when you have a small group of people who are loyal, or very active, or spend a really long time on the site. They are doing much more than the average user, so it makes a bump.

Find out what motivates them and make more of it!

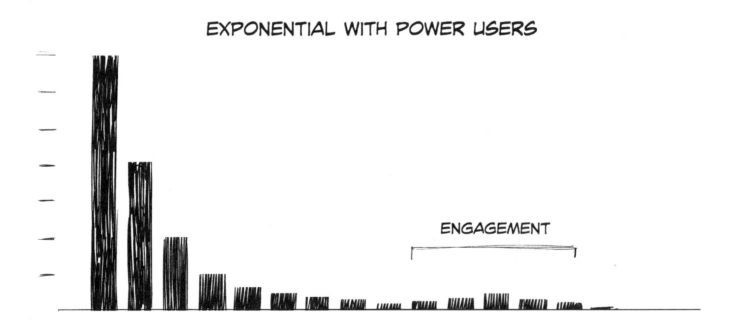

EXPONENTIAL WITH POWER USERS

ENGAGEMENT

THIS SHOWS A SMALL GROUP OF PEOPLE, WHO ARE DOING A LOT.

Exponential with Conversion Problem

A huge drop between two bars often indicates a barrier for users.

You want your "slide" to look gentle and smooth. If it has any insane drops or rough spots, those indicate problems. If the home page of your site is really confusing, you might get a graph like this because very few people will get to the second page. A/B tests are a really effective way to find the problem, if it isn't obvious.

EXPONENTIAL WITH CONVERSION PROBLEM

BIG DROP=
BIG PROBLEM

A HUGE GAP BETWEEN TWO BARS OFTEN INDICATES A BARRIER FOR USERS.

Stats—Sessions versus Users

A user can visit more than once. The difference between the visitors (unique users) and their visits (sessions) says a lot about loyalty and engagement.

Let's say I visit your website. I spend a few minutes there, I have a good time, everybody is happy. After, we all give each other (virtual) high fives, and I leave.

Then, tomorrow I visit again. And the next day, I go again.

I have been there three times—three *sessions*—but I am only one guy. One really handsome guy, but still. Just one.

If I were your only visitor (a sad situation in itself) you would see "3 sessions" and "1 user" in your Google Analytics, or maybe "3 Visitors" and "1 Unique Visitor" in other analytics products.

They're not saying I am more unique than your other visitors, although I'll take it as a compliment anyway. A *unique* visitor is a single user, a person, who can visit more than once.

Everything Is Relative

Try not to get excited or depressed about the actual numbers. You might be tempted to say things like, "Is three sessions good?" but that's the wrong way to look at it.

For you, 3,000 sessions might be the biggest day ever, and for some sites *3 million* is still depressing. It's all relative.

Instead, ask yourself: Is three sessions better than last month? How many users did you need to get that many sessions? And is *that* better than last month? Is that what a product like yours should do?

These numbers mean more together.

You should spend your time looking at, and thinking about, the relationship between the sessions and users numbers. It tells you a bit about loyalty and about how well you turn *first-time* visitors into *repeat* visitors.

Analytics are not your score, they are a story. You just have to know how to read them.

A User Is Actually a Device. Wait, What?!

As far as I know, analytics can't know that your phone and your laptop are both controlled by the human that I affection-ately call "you."

So, if I visit your site three times on my laptop and then two more times on my phone, you will see "5 sessions" and "2 *users*" in Google Analytics, even though both of those users are controlled by the human I affectionately call "me."

There isn't anything you can do about it; it's just good to know. The downside is this: you can never know exactly how many individual humans came to your site. The upside is this: you can do a little more digging into how often users return on different devices.

Stats—New versus Return Visitors

You will have many first-time visitors, and some of them will come back. By separating them into groups, you can start to understand the health of your site and what makes people return.

The "health" of your site is general metaphor I have used a lot in meetings with clients and bosses. Basically, it is the combination of many statistics that indicate whether things are getting "better" or "worse" overall.

Return visitors and new visitors tell a big part of that story. They are like taking your site's pulse.

New Visitors

When a user comes to your site for the first time, they know nothing. They might come from an ad, or a link on a blog, or they might have searched for something relevant (or irrelevant) and discovered you by chance.

Either way, they're new.

Return Visitors

If that new visitor comes back a second time (or third, or hundredth), they are a "return" visitor. This is important, because now they know what your site is and hopefully they recognize it.

> **NOTE**
>
> It is still possible that the user came from an ad, or a link on a blog, or they searched for something to find you again. But they also might have come back by choice.

These numbers mean more together.

Like most of these analytics, the real information comes from comparing the two numbers. This time we want to know the percentage of each, because if you add all the new users and all the returning users, that's all the users. Math is fun!

> **REMEMBER**
>
> If a *percentage* goes down, it doesn't mean you have less of something. It just means that number represents a smaller piece of the pie. It might have gone down because the other number went up! Or, maybe both went up, but the other number went up more!

Try to balance growth and loyalty.

Early in the growth of your site, it's actually good to have *mostly* new users. It means you're being discovered a lot. Maybe 10 to 20% returning visitors, but that's just a rough guideline.

Over time (months or years), your goal is to make the numbers shift the other way, without losing "sessions and users."

A very established site will have *mostly* return visitors, and more like 20 to 30% new visitors.

If you have very few return visitors, that's a problem because nobody is coming back.

If you have very few new visitors, that's a problem because nobody is finding you.

Stats—Pageviews

Is your site/app a tool that needs to be efficient? Or, do you have a site that needs to be engaging? Pageviews can tell different stories.

A *"pageview" is pretty much what it sounds like:* a user viewed a specific page on your website (or app).

Pageviews are a *passive* measurement, because users doesn't have to *do* anything other than see the page.

They probably clicked or tapped something to get to that page, to view it, but analytics will count the page view even if the user leaves their apartment as the page loads, and they get lost in the woods, only to meet and fall in love with a bear and live happily ever after in the woods, never having actually seen the page.

"View" might not be the best description. Think of it as a page "load."

Lots of pageviews can be good or bad. Or both.

If you are Google, then having a lot of pageviews is bad, because Google wants you to find the right search result as fast as possible and go to it. Nobody wants to go through pages and pages of search results.

So, for Google Search, *fewer* pageviews is better.

On the other hand, Facebook would probably strap a screen to your eyeballs if it could, so you would never *stop* viewing pages. For them, *more* pageviews is better.

If your site makes money by showing banners on each page, then more pageviews is good because you make more money.

However, this also creates a reason to force users to view more pages than necessary (ever seen a 10-photo gallery broken into 10 individual pages?), which is a bad experience.

When there is a business reason to do something, and a UX reason *not* to do it, you have to be careful. If you can, fix that problem completely.

If you can't fix it, remember: the more you make users work for your content, the less content they will see.

If you're only doing UX to show more ads, you're making the world worse, not better.

Stats—Time

Time and pageviews have some similarities, but unlike pageviews, time metrics can tell you where your users are engaged... or confused.

Time per Visit (or time per session) is how long users spend in your app or on your site, *on average*.

Time per Page tells you how long users spend on each specific page or screen, *on average*.

When you are using averages from many users, you have to remember that there is probably a wide variety of times people spend on the site or on a page. By *averaging* those times it gives you an idea of how the site is performing overall and allows you to compare one page to another page.

For example, suppose that your site has an average Time per Visit of three seconds. That means users are either finding what they need extremely quickly or nobody stays long enough to do anything at all.

If you're Google, you might try to give people what they're looking for as fast as possible.

If you're Wikipedia, three seconds per visit is bad, because nobody can read an article in three seconds.

If you compare two pages and one has an average Time per Page of 45 seconds,

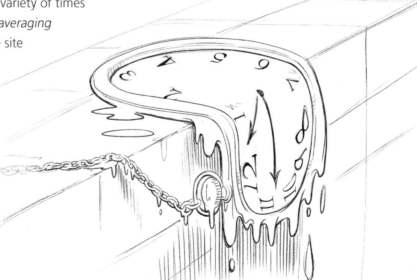

and the other has 3 minutes, then those two pages are performing much differently.

Don't Assume That Time Is Good

When users are *confused* they will also spend longer on a page, because they are trying to figure it out.

More time can mean more engagement or it can mean your menu is confusing, or the registration form is too difficult.

Compare Time and Other Stats to Learn More

How much time and how many pages can tell you a lot about user behavior. There is no combination that is "good" or "bad"—it depends on what your design is supposed to do.

If your site has a lot of text, like the *New York Times*, then you probably want people to spend more time on fewer pages—they are reading! Lots of pages in a short time might mean they are browsing, searching, or lost.

If your site is all images, like Pinterest, then you probably want a short Time per Page, on a lot of pages, because images are quick and easy to *consume*—users are browsing! But you still want a long Time per Visit—that's exploring!

If you're Google you probably want very *low* Time per Visit, Time per Page, and Pageviews, because that would indicate that people are finding good results quickly.

If you're Facebook you want very *high* Time per Visit (engagement) and Pageviews (ads), but Time per Page is not very relevant.

Stats—Bounce Rate and Exit Rate

It is valuable to know about the users who don't stay on your site, and which parts of your design make people to leave.

Bounce rate is the percentage of users who arrive at your site, but don't come in. They "bounce off" instead of actually *using* it.

No clicks. Nothing. Nada.

A low bounce rate (10 to 30%) is good because bouncing is bad. A high bounce rate (70 to 99%) is bad. Everything in the middle is normal-ish. Not good, not terrible, not interesting.

Your bounce will *never* be zero. *Somebody* always bounces. If it is zero percent (or even less than five percent), ask your developers to check the code for a technical error. You might be measuring your bounce rate incorrectly.

Your goal is to make bounce rate as low as possible.

The most common causes of high bounce rates are designs that aren't trustworthy,

headlines that are bad or unexpected, confusing IA, and designs that don't show the user where to click.

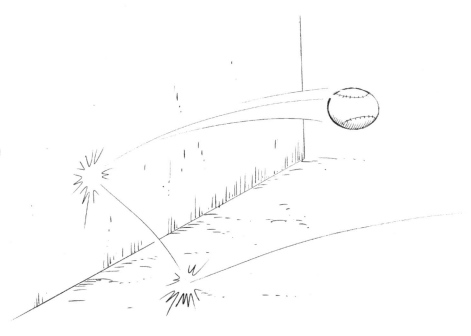

Exit Rate

Every user will leave your site eventually. That is called an *exit*.

The exit rate of a page tells you what percentage of the visitors left the site after viewing *that* page.

If you only have three pages, then on average, 33% of users will exit from each one. If you have 10 pages, on average 10% will exit from each one.

The more users go to a page, the higher the exit rate might be.

Look for pages with exit rates that "stick out." If it is much higher or lower than the others, look into it. It might be a dead end, or a difficult form, or it could even be a good thing!

I once redesigned a travel site with one-of-a-kind travel packages. Crazy stuff that you couldn't find anywhere else. One package had a much *lower* exit rate than the others, even though the page designs were identical. When I looked closer, I realized that the content was written in a different style; it was more exciting! By changing the style of the other packages to match, we got users to stay for three minutes longer and two more pages per visit!

The Probabilities of Interaction

Uncertainty is part of your UX life. It's not a yes/no thing. You're not trying to make something work, you are trying to make it work *better.*

When you measure user behavior, it helps to understand what a group looks like, statistically. Numbers can tell you a lot about your design, but you need the right perspective. UX is about increasing the chance, the odds, the *probability* that users will do something.

Think of UX as the process of reducing the number of options in a user's mental roulette wheel. Every user may not win every time, but more users will win overall.

1% of People Will Do Anything

Many years ago, after many discussions about user-generated content, a colleague of mine named a rule after me:

Marsh's Law: *"Every feature will eventually be abused to its maximum abusability."*

Or, you can think about it like this: if something can be used, it will eventually be used by *someone.*

That doesn't make it *good.*

On a page with 25 banners that nobody cares about, a few people will still click them.

On a site with eight levels of navigation, the deepest pages will still be visited once or twice.

And I am still amazed that Facebook "Like" buttons get clicks on porn sites—or so I have heard.

It will be tempting to keep features because some users use it. Resist that temptation.

Every time someone clicks a shitty feature, they aren't clicking something more useful.

90% Is Everybody

If you make a design so effective that the majority of people do what you hoped, that's great!

If 90% of your users are aware that they can pay or register to get an upgrade, your design is great.

If 90% of users leave your site without clicking anything, it's an emergency.

The only time I have seen 100% of users do something, it was a technical error or there was only one user.

Probabilities Are Not Intuitive

If 10% of people click on your landing page, and then 80% of those people make a purchase, is the design good?

Actually, no.

Many people will look at the conversion rate and say "Wow! 80% of our users make a purchase!"

Then, the whole team will go have drinks, or play in the inflatable castle, or whatever it is people do at your company to celebrate.

However, as the UX designer, you should not go to that party. You're losing about 90% of potential sales.

But you aren't losing them in the checkout. You are losing them at the landing page.

If 40% of people click on the landing page and 40% of them make a purchase, you would actually sell *twice as much*, even though your conversion rate is *half.*

80% of 10% = 8%

40% of 40% = 16%

Almost every company I have worked with has had a problem like this, but very few people notice. It can literally be a *million-dollar mistake.*

Structure versus Choice

There are two major aspects of UX design that can give you mysterious results: IA and user psychology. And it is possible for one to look like the other.

We have already learned a lot about the ways you can present information so more people choose certain options than they normally would.

But what if you see a lot of people choosing an option that you didn't want them to choose?

There are probably a million examples of this. However, my goal in this lesson is not to give you a library of scenarios—just to give you a taste of the way your navigation or layout might be a sheep in psychology's clothing.

Order versus Appeal

You have learned about how to bias your content so that certain options look more attractive than others.

If users don't choose those options it is possible you did it wrong. Or, you might just have them in the wrong order.

Items on the left of a horizontal list or at the top of a vertical list get more clicks because they are the first things people see.

Anchoring only works when the anchor is the first option. If you have something else in the first position, it might be getting clicks just because users see it first.

I have seen people build strategies on the assumption that Option #1 is what users like most, when in reality it is just what users see first.

Content Attention versus Surface Attention

You have learned how to grab the user's attention and how to minimize competing messages.

So what if everybody loves your site, but nobody reads it?

A common trend lately is websites with _amazing visual effects_ and _animations as you scroll_. The problem is this: sometimes, it is more interesting to scroll up and down than to stop and read.

That's _surface_ attention. We want _content_ attention.

Animations and cool effects should be used as elements of delight, not the whole design. Remember that motion beats everything, attention-wise. That means people will watch whatever is moving and ignore whatever isn't.

Ever tried to _read_ moving text? Probably not, because you were too busy _watching_ it.

Motion and _parallax effects_ should draw attention to things the user should do. Not the pure awesomeness of the designer's imagination.

Hierarchy versus Motivation

We have learned that user psychology is about motivating users to do important actions, like registering, buying, subscribing, upgrading, etc.

If you're not getting much traffic to your conversion pages, it could be because people don't want to register. Or, it could be because the users can't get there.

If a user clicks down into a page that doesn't have a "Register" button on it, they will not go backward when they become motivated to register.

They just won't find the button.

Very few users will ever mention it, because it's not a visual problem. It's a business problem.

A/B Tests

User research and user psychology are great ways to predict how users will behave and what they will do. But we don't just want to predict. We want to *know*.

Let me paint the picture a little bit first...

Imagine that you want to design a page to sell shoes. And, of course, you want to sell as many shoes as possible. What do you think would get more people to buy?

A video of the shoes?

Complete shipping details before they click "buy"?

The logo of the shoe brand?

A money-back guarantee?

How do you choose?

If your first thought was, "Ask the users!" that's not a bad idea. But often—when the options are all subjective, like this—asking people just confirms that different people like different things.

So, how can you decide between subjective things, like a boss?!

Design all the things! Then, you launch all the options at the same time, as an A/B Test.

What Is an A/B Test?

An A/B test is a way of asking thousands or millions of real visitors which option is best.

The tests make sure that each unique visitor only sees one option. Then, after enough people have gone through your test, you can see which version of the design created more clicks. The test should also measure the "confidence level" statistically so you know when you're done (don't stop it too early!)

You can do it with 2 versions, or 20 versions. Just remember: only part of your traffic can see each one, so the more versions you are testing, the more traffic or time you will need.

Some tips

1. A/B Testing is usually free, other than the time it takes to design and create the pages you're testing. The results can be extremely valuable, so even a small cost to do an A/B Test is very worth it.

2. It is not the same thing as launching a new page and then watching to see if that page seems better than the old one. The *only* way to compare two designs is to run them both at the *same time*, using (roughly) equal numbers of people for both.

3. An A/B Test is most reliable when you *only change one detail*. If two pages are the same, but one has red links and one has blue links, that's fine. If they also have different menus, then there is no way to tell whether it is the link color or the menu that is making the difference. If you want to test multiple changes, you need a *multivariate test* (next lesson!).

4. Testing two totally different pages, like a home page and a checkout form, is useless. That's not a proper A/B Test.

A Multi-what-now Test?!

An A/B test is brilliant for testing a specific change in your design. But, if you want to test how one design element affects another, you need a *multivariate test.*

A multivariate test can test combinations of changes.

Multi-VARIATE. (Say: "multi-very-it")

When you change one thing on your page or site, it can affect how the users think about something else. A multivariate test allows you to test *relationships* between design elements.

Let's say you have three options for headlines:

Headline 1: "This is the greatest thing ever!"

Headline 2: "This is the worst thing ever!"

Headline 3: "This is kind of really ok, ish!"

And you also have three options for photos to go with those headlines!

Photo 1: A puppy.

Photo 2: A hamburger.

Photo 3: Your mom.

That doesn't sound so bad. Seems like an A/B/C test. Right?

Nope.

Here's the kicker:

Any of the headlines will work with any of the photos. But depending on the combination, the user might have different reactions.

Maybe some people want to see the greatest thing ever, but only if the photo shows something they like.

Maybe some people would love to see the worst thing ever, but only if the photos show something they hate.

Or, maybe your mom makes every headline more effective! Who knows?!

Very subjective. Very complicated.

How would you know what combination to use!?

A multivariate test, that's how.

Multivariate tests think harder than you can.

In this case there are **nine** combinations of photos and headlines:

Headline 1 with photo 1, 2 or 3.

Headline 2 with photo 1, 2, or 3.

And headline 3 with photo 1, 2, or 3.

That is a lot of information to compare in your head. You will never be able to make a rational guess about which combination of headline and photo will be most popular.

So don't!

Let the software pick combinations of headlines and photos randomly, and at the end it will tell you that Headline 2 with Photo 3 got the highest percentage of clicks. Or Headline 1 and Photo 1. Or whatever.

Multivariate tests need more traffic than an A/B test because there are more combinations to test, but they also produce answers that would be a pain in the ass using A/B testing.

Try it!

Sometimes A/B Testing Is the Only Way to Know

This book includes a lot of ways that you can use psychology to make things look and feel better than they would otherwise. But what if you have to choose between two psychological strategies?

Eventually you will come to a design choice that is psychology versus psychology; motivation versus motivation; emotion versus emotion.

Maybe you have to choose between creating trust in your company or creating trust in the product you're selling.

Maybe you have to choose between promoting the exclusive status of the brand or the popularity of the brand.

Maybe you need to choose between the word "enjoy" and the word "save"—they are both benefits! Or are they?

In those situations, it is damn near impossible to base your decisions on theory. And asking users face to face is not reliable unless you plan to ask 10,000 of them.

Sometimes A/B testing is the only way to know.

Design and launch the experiment. Make the versions exactly the same except for that psychological detail.

Compare the results, and go with the winner.

Do the science. Trust the science. Be the science.

XIV

Get a Job, You Dirty Hippy

What Does a UX Designer Do All Day?

Your first day at work as a UX designer will be very exciting or terrifying, depending on your personality. But don't worry; this is what you can expect.

On a typical day I will arrive late, my personal secretary will give me a vanilla latté just the way I like it, and there is a waiting room full of people that want me to bestow knowledge upon them.

But I like to ignore them for a while when I come in so they recognize my importance. I put my feet up on my desk, sip my latté, and then—if I feel like it—I will see each of my minions for five minutes, so they get a chance to worship my wireframes, kiss my ring, and shuffle out of the room backward, while they bow and say "sorry" over and over.

Pretty much what you expected, right?

You wish.

REALITY CHECK

As a professional UX designer, you will spend most of your time gathering information or explaining things to people who may or may not agree with you.

UX is a very valuable part of any team. You will have a lot of responsibility, and you will probably get paid a salary that reflects your value. UX is also a role that will not be understood by most of your colleagues, and therefore you might be surprised how often they want your input, and/or don't listen to it.

Different UX Jobs Are Different

Depending on the type of clients you have, the type of projects you do, the type of company you work in, and whether it's a poor company or a rich company, your calendar will change. But since you asked, this is what you might spend your time on, based on my not-even-slightly-scientific analysis of years working with startups, agencies, and in-house teams.

Internal meetings (mostly unnecessary)	30%
Documenting designs	10%
Sketching/wireframes	10%
Facebook/internal chat (Skype, Slack, etc.)	7%
Discussing requirements and feedback	6%
"Coffee breaks"	6%
Watching funny videos sent by colleagues	5%
Analyzing data/research	5%
Discussing designs with developers	3%
Presenting insights to bosses/clients	3%
Reviewing analytics	3%
Saying *yes* to things when the answer should be *no*	2%
Staring out the window, thinking	2%
Reading UX blogs	2%
Feeling like the Wizard of Oz	1%
Doing face-to-face user research	1%
Being micromanaged by a nondesigner	1%
Expressing yourself artistically	0.99%
Expressing yourself violently	0.9%
Getting people to agree that true facts are true	0.5%
Bragging to colleagues about your salary	0.5%
Explaining why "a chance to win an iPad" is stupid	0.1%
Winning awards	0.01%

Which UX Job Is Right For You?

All UX-related designers work on the same sorts of things, but different jobs focus on different areas. Which one is best for you?

If you ever want to start a heated argument, go into a room full of UX designers and ask, "What is the definition of UX?" I promise you, all hell will break loose.

UX is a word like "personality." Everybody understands what it is until somebody tries to define it in specific terms, and then the pitchforks come out.

With that in mind, I also understand that beginners need to know which jobs to look for, which jobs exist, and which jobs will make you happy. Following is a very brief overview of UX roles, which hopefully won't make anybody want to send me death threats.

UI versus UX

First of all UI and UX are very different jobs. If you ever see a job where the job title is "UI/UX" it means the company doesn't know what UX is, or it's trying to cover two roles with one salary. Beware.

The User Interface (UI) is what you see. UX is why you see it.

If you're more excited by making beautiful apps, or working with branding and ad campaigns, or designing logos and icons and color schemes, UI is for you.

If you're more interested in what this book contains, UX is more your style. (But you're always welcome to learn both!)

Generalist versus Specialist

You might hear UXers and recruiters talking about "general" UX (a little of everything) or "specialist" UX (focus on one of the roles described in this lesson).

In my opinion, *all beginners should be generalists*. Try everything. Learn everything. Take any responsibility someone is willing to give you.

Five years from now, when you're pretty good at most parts of UX, *then* you can decide if you want to be *great* at one particular area.

Information Architecture

Information Architects work mostly with the structure of the content and pages. In smaller projects like apps and basic websites, Information Architecture (IA) is not a huge job, so it isn't a separate role. But in really big projects like a global corporate intranet, or something like Wikipedia, or social networks, or large government archives, IA can be a big deal.

If that feels like your thing, then the role of Information Architect is for you.

Interaction Design

Interaction Design (IxD) is the interface itself, but without thinking too much about style. So, you might not work as much with the IA, but you will get deeper into the details of animations, flows, and layouts for the actual pages.

IxD tends to connect more with frontend coding or UI design because it's hard to think about one without thinking about the other. So if that sounds like you, then maybe IxD is your role of choice.

UX

UX is the general term, or the "umbrella," that all of these roles are "within". If you don't want to focus, and would prefer to be more of a *big picture* designer, then just stick with UX as a role. I have been doing this stuff for a while now and I still prefer UX as a job title.

UX will interact more with other departments than specialist UX roles like IA or IxD, and it might include more of the business considerations. So, if you think more about the *product* rather than the interface itself, UX is probably more your style.

UX Strategy

It's hard to explain what a UX Strategy is in one paragraph, but think of it as a combination of marketing and UX. This type of position is more common in bigger, tech-savvy companies or digital agencies. Those products and features need to fit into a marketing plan rather than solving real-world problems as a product.

i.e., If you're making an app for a company whose product is alcohol, it's more *strategic* than useful, because nothing digital will make their alcohol better. Still cool, still UX, but it's different.

If you want to be a "Growth Hacker," or if you want to build UX into marketing campaigns, or if you want to be a less technical (but more advertising-oriented) version of a UX designer, this might be your deal.

UX Research

The opposite side of the UX coin (compared to UX Strategy) might be UX Research. These people do way more face-to-face user interviews and spend much more time with the data than a generalist like me.

If you *love* analysis and want to spend a lot more time solving real-world user problems—and probably be a little more scientific—this is a good role for you.

Agency, In-House, or Startup?

The type of company you work for will also affect your role. Officially, I recommend that you try working at all of these types of companies if you can. They will teach you different things.

Agency

As a consultant, like ad agencies or UX agencies, you will see a lot more projects, and many different types of projects, and speed matters. That means you will learn faster, it can be more exciting, and your experience will be more diverse.

However, at an agency you will only spend three to six months on a typical project, and most often there won't be a "version 2" of anything, so you won't get a chance to live with a product or think *long term.*

In-House

When you are part of the team *inside* a company, you will work mostly on a single product or a set of products, all the time. You will learn a deeper understanding of that type of user and that type of product, and you will probably work on several versions of it. In-house teams often get to "try" more things, and A/B testing is where you will learn a lot about individual features and tactics.

However, in-house teams tend to work on the same types of things for a long time, so your experience won't be as diverse, and you won't be as "deep" in other areas.

Startup

At a startup, you will get an exciting opportunity and will probably have an influence on every part of the company. Since there won't be many designers, you will get a lot more responsibility. Sometimes, the best learning happens when you bite off a little more than you can chew.

However, at a startup you might not have a boss with UX experience, so you're on your own. That means you get more glory when it goes right, but you could also ruin the product if you're not careful. And you probably won't have any money to spend, so anything more expensive than "free" will be too expensive. That is more difficult, but if you're creative it might also generate your best ideas.

What Goes in a UX Portfolio?

UX is still relatively new, and difficult for nondesigners to understand. When you apply for a job you need to inform and inspire.

Remember your audience: they don't understand UX.

The average "boss" that is interviewing you for a UX position won't actually know a lot about UX. Or, at least, that's what you should assume.

Begin your portfolio by saying what you do or what responsibilities you are interested in. It might not be a bad idea to say what *you* believe you are going to add, as well.

If your future boss is a UX wizard, they will appreciate your clarity and the fact that you took the time to explain it in a simple way.

If they are regular people, it will help them understand what to ask you about, and why your portfolio might not include many "pretty things."

Tell Short, Visual Stories

A UX portfolio doesn't have the luxury of showing lots of beautiful screenshots. If you *can* make sexy interfaces, too, then great. If not, then you have to tell stories about what you have done.

Make it simple and short. If the boss wants details, they can ask you for them in the interview. For now, explain what you did, why you did it, how you researched it, and any of the limitations you had to work with.

And even though UX isn't about style, you *should* have visual things to show: sketches, wireframes, analytics screenshots, site maps, before-and-after designs, etc.

Show your process! Teach them what you do!

Focus on Problems, Insights, and Results

If you focus on the pictures, it will give the boss the impression that you mostly do pictures. So don't.

Every project you do can be summarized as a problem that you discovered through research, a solution that was supported by evidence, data and your ingenious insights about users, and the results of that solution—hopefully good results.

If you prove that you can make things *work* better by understanding users, you will immediately look valuable to any organization, regardless of how much experience you have.

No Experience? Make Some!

Unlike most jobs, it's not that hard to make a basic UX portfolio without any real jobs or clients.

Do case studies: Take a famous product or website—maybe even the one you want to work for—and get some real people to use it while you observe. Design a concept that solves some of the problems that you discover, or design A/B tests to investigate. Explain all of your reasoning, show your work, and make a wireframe for the final solution.

Solve a real problem: Design a mobile app to solve a problem you see in the world. It doesn't have to be a full-sized startup pitch… just demonstrate that you can produce solutions by yourself. That's very attractive to a potential boss.

A/B-test your own site: Have a blog or a personal site somewhere online? You should. Google Analytics allows you to do A/B tests for free using a product called Content Experiments, so do some tests and see what happens. Then put the results in your portfolio.

Be Yourself

Don't be afraid to add some personality! When employers sit and read 100 applications for a design position, there is nothing more interesting than someone who seems smart and unique.

Have a blog? Link to it!

Do photography? Show some!

Does your background give you a unique perspective? Mention it!

Nobody expects a beginner to have a lot of experience. Show them you are smart, can solve problems, and that you're willing to do the work; the rest is just details.

This brings us to the end of the book. 100 lessons! Well done!

UX is 90% about how you think, and 10% about what you design. If you have read every lesson, understood them, and feel like you can apply them to real products, you're already doing well.

I am pretty sarcastic a lot of the time, but UX is something I am really passionate about, and I hope this book has made it easy to share some of that passion with you.

You are always welcome to find me on Twitter: *@JoelMarsh*.

I also blog about UX and share links to the best things I find: *www.TheHipperElement.com*.

Thanks for reading, and good luck!

Index

A

Absolut Vodka, readability of label on, 180
A/B tests
    about, 217–218, 221
    collecting user data with, 195
    finding problems with, 203
accessibility, usability and, 168–169
accountability, creating trust and, 107
adaptive design, 150
addiction, conditioning and, 99–101
affiliation, as motivation, 36, 40
agency consultants, 229
air/water/food, as motivation, 35
alignment, in visual design, 121
analysis, as ingredient of UX, 5
analytics, 194–195
anchoring, 72, 215
animation
    motion and, 123
    visual effects and, 215–216
appeal vs. order, 215
apps, flows of, 91
Ariely, Dan, Ted Talk about decision-making,
    75

associations, 98
attention of users, getting, 76–77
average person, 193
axis of interaction, in layouts, 143–144

B

back button, users using, 92
bad UX vs. good UX, 166
bandwagon effect, 72
bar graphs, 196
beauty, usability and, 159
behavior, shaping, 100
beliefs, user, 29
big text, getting attention of users with, 76
blog, UX, 231
bounce rate, 211
brand vs. UX copywriting, 172–173
browsing, usability and, 162
business
    goals aligned with user goals, 14–15
    process and UX designer process, 16–17
buttons, 92, 148–149, 176, 182

C

Call-To-Action (CTA) formula, 174–175
card-sorting, in user research, 56, 62–63
categories, information architecture type, 87
champions, choosing, 43
choice
    illusion of, 74–75
    structure vs., 215–216
classical conditioning, 99
clicks, not counting in flows, 91
closed/direct questions, 55
closing deal, during interaction (persuasion
        formula), 182
cognitive biases
    hyperbolic discounting in, 80–81
    in questions, 72–73
cognitive load, usability equals, 158–159
color
    getting attention of users with contrast
        and, 77
    in visual design, 114–115
    wireframes and, 130
columns, adjusting width of, 181
common sense, 70